Carrascolendas:
Bilingual Education
Through Television

Frederick Williams
Geraldine Van Wart
foreword by
Senator Ralph Yarborough

The Praeger Special Studies program—utilizing the most modern and efficient book production techniques and a selective worldwide distribution network—makes available to the academic, government, and business communities significant, timely research in U.S. and international economic, social, and political development.

Carrascolendas:
Bilingual Education
Through Television

104308

PRAEGER SPECIAL STUDIES IN U.S. ECONOMIC, SOCIAL, AND POLITICAL ISSUES

Praeger Publishers   New York   Washington   London

Library of Congress Cataloging in Publication Data

Williams, Frederick, 1933-
  Carrascolendas.

  (Praeger special studies in U.S. economic, social,
and political issues)
  Includes bibliographical references.
  1. Carrascolendas. 2. Education, Bilingual—United
States. 3. Mexican-Americans—Education. I. Van
Wart, Geraldine, joint author. II. Title.
LC6579.C37W54   371.9'7   74-1738
ISBN 0-275-08780-8

PRAEGER PUBLISHERS
111 Fourth Avenue, New York, N.Y. 10003, U.S.A.
5, Cromwell Place, London SW7 2JL, England

Published in the United States of America in 1974
by Praeger Publishers, Inc.

Printed in the United States of America

"Carrascolendas" is the name of a bilingual (Spanish-English) educational television program for children that originated in 1970 at the studios of Educational Television KLRN on the campus of The University of Texas at Austin. So wonderfully successful the program proved, that it won six regional and national awards in three years, capped by winning for the United States, for its first win in the field, the UNICEF prize at the Japan Prize International Educational Program Contest in Tokyo in October 1973.

The idea for the project was conceived by Aida Barrera of The University of Texas Communication Center; Ms. Barrera is now Executive Producer of this imaginative and stimulating series. She suggested that it be named "Carrascolendas" from a legendary former name of her mother's home, Rio Grande City. That legend was history. In 1748-53 Colonel Jose de Escandor, Spanish born, reared, and married, was planting colonies along the vacant northeastern Rio Grande frontier of New Spain. A little Spanish town of Carnestolendas ("Carnival") was a part of his 1753 settlement. Nearly a hundred years later, after its name had evolved into Carrascolendas, it became a shipping point on the Rio Grande to supply General Taylor's army in Mexico and merged into the wartime boom town, its name becoming Rio Grande City. Now, more than a century later, Carrascolendas, revived, is a little Spanish town on television, evolved into a bilingual town of great imagery and charm.

My own interest in bilingual education began in El Paso, Texas while I was a young lawyer, noting the need for education among Mexican-American children, but not knowing how to meet it. Years later, Monroe Sweetland, legislative consultant of the western states for the National Education Association, invited me to a Tucson Conference (1966), and explained what was needed. In January 1967 I introduced in the United States Senate the first bilingual education bill ever introduced in the United States Congress. Being on both the Senate Appropriations Committee and the Education Subcommittee, I was privileged to see it written into law within 12 months. With this stamp of national congressional approval, bilingual education for the educationally deprived received a great boost.

"Carrascolendas," a most perceptive use of educational television, has given bilingual education another great boost. This is the type of productive and successful use from which teachers and scholars receive their great rewards, those of the spirit and intellect.

Ralph W. Yarborough
Austin, Texas

PREFACE

As this book goes to press, those of us who participated in the early years of "Carrascolendas" can be proud to note that it has now won eight major program awards, including two international ones. It is also noteworthy that in 1973-74 the project was continued by funding from the National Center for Educational Technology, U.S. Office of Education. This new project has stimulated several major innovations in "Carrascolendas"—the development of a half-hour story "theme" to replace the segmented format, and the extension of audience and programming materials to other Spanish-speaking Americans, namely Puerto Ricans and Cubans. In short, the inhabitants of "Carrascolendas" are alive and well and can probably be seen on any television station with an interest in public and bilingual/bicultural programming.

We owe a note of recognition to Dr. Diana Natalicio, of the University of Texas at El Paso, for her work on the first year of the project, the report of which is incorporated in this volume.

As demonstration of our confidence in bilingual television programming, we have donated any authors' income from this book to station KRLN for use in this area.

Contents

LIST OF TABLES

LIST OF FIGURES

Carrascolendas:
Bilingual Education
Through Television

TELEVISION WITH
BEHAVIORAL OBJECTIVES

It is no new thought that television can be a powerful educational tool. In the last score or so years we have seen a great variety of applications often referred to as educational (ETV) or instructional (ITV) television. But it has only been in the last half dozen years that propects for using public television for the education of young children have achieved such widespread attention. Most of this attention is due to the interest aroused by "Sesame Street." To many, the contribution of this program to the advancement of educational broadcasting is the idea of using mixtures of entertainment and instruction to reach a great variety of preschool children. But to those of us working in such projects, it is a successful example of how the behavioral goals and strategies of educational planners, the creativity of television producers and artists, and the investigative skills of the researchers can be combined as a most powerful educational tool.

"Carrascolendas" is a children's television program, but it is distinctive in that it is culturally targeted and bilingual in Spanish and English. The research conducted in conjunction with the development of this program is the topic of this monograph. The key theme in summarizing these efforts is to describe the steps in the development and evaluation of the program series. The hope is that new projects of this type may benefit from our experiences or, at best, avoid our mistakes.

PLANNING WITH OBJECTIVES

Among the lessons learned from the success of "Sesame Street" as well as the first three years of "Carrascolendas" is the critical role played by behavioral (instructional) objectives. As used within the field of education, behavioral objectives are precise descriptions of what one expects to occur as the result of instruction. They are specifications of what we intend to teach, defined in terms of behavior we should be able to observe in pupils. Behavioral objectives are the criteria whereby educational practices may be evaluated. This concept of objectives and the method for specifying them have been of critical importance in the planning, management, and evaluation of such programs as "Sesame Street," the more recent "The Electric Company," and are a key topic in this report on "Carrascolendas." Behavioral objectives provide a basis for the following:

1. to define the specific instructional needs of a given target population;

2. to express the precise aims of a television series where assumptions can be made about the needs and existing capabilities of the audience;

3. to provide the basis for unambiguous communication about programming aims, which is necessary for the cooperation of educational planners, television writers, producers, and directors;

4. to provide precise criteria by which the formative evaluation of any newly produced television segment may be gauged, where the researchers' measures and the producer's objectives have the same definition;

5. to provide for the summative evaluation of an entire program series; to measure the degree to which a variety of objectives are achieved;

6. to use as a basis for subsequent planning of a series relative to specific needs of a population and to known effects of a prior program series;

7. to facilitate content assessment analysis where the variations in content or strategy may be studied relative to achievement of objectives; and

8. to be a basis for cost analysis of the materials of instruction relative to objectives achieved in specific numbers of pupils.

As can be seen from the above list, the use of objectives facilitates the integration of the research aspects in almost all stages of planning development and evaluation of an educational television series. The researchers' planning is tied to the definition of the needs and abilities of the target population. In educational circles, this is called "baseline data," in that it identifies a starting point from which the objectives of a series are built upon. In the planning phases of a series, the researcher may be a chief consultant on the selection of objectives that will be contained in the series and on the definition of those items. It is important that goals be worded so that they may be evaluated later. During the production process, the prototype version of program sections may be pretested. The criteria for the evaluation are the previously stated behavioral objectives. Research of this type, done during the development of the series to provide enroute guidance to the producer, is known as _formative_ evaluation. Finally, there is an evaluation to assess the effects of the series relative to its goals, a process known as _summative_ evaluation.

SOME NOTES ON "SESAME STREET"

The development of "Sesame Street" represented a number of innovative examples in the integration of research strategies throughout the planning, production, and evaluation stages.[1] Within the broad goals of entertainment, intellectual development, and cultural development, a variety of behavioral objectives was identified for the three-to-five-year-old target population. Simply delimiting the target audience for a series of this type was an innovation. Given the identification of behavioral objectives, expert evaluation was sought to be sure that such objectives were stated in terms of behavioral goals— that is, in terms of specifications that could be readily observed and measured. Along with the identification of behavioral goals, specific instruments were developed to measure children's progress vis-à-vis these goals. Evaluation was then a matter of determining whether children who viewed the program exhibited the behaviors that were the specified objectives of the series. It was the evaluators' job to select samples of children and to apply instruments that would gauge these behaviors.

In the first summative evaluation of "Sesame Street," the following main questions were posed:
1. Do viewers learn more than nonviewers?
2. Of the viewers, which children learn least, and which children learn most?
3. What is the show's effectiveness among subgroups (for example, boy-girl, lower-middle class, high-low achievers, Spanish-English speakers?)
4. Which elements of the format are most effective?

The summative evaluation design involved sampling these four populations of children, with emphasis on the first type: (1) disadvantaged, inner city; (2) advantaged, suburban; (3) advantaged and disadvantaged, rural; and (4) disadvantaged, Spanish-speaking.

Site selections were limited by three criteria. The area had to be served by a VHF (rather than UHF) educational television station; the station had to agree to telecast "Sesame Street" at either 9 a.m. or 10 a.m. daily; the site had to contain a large enough number of children of the first population type. The five sites finally chosen were Boston; Durham, N.C.; Phoenix; suburban Philadelphia; and a ten-county rural area in northeastern California.

3

In the first stage of sampling, the representative social classes were comprised of lower-socioeconomic-status (SES) children in urban areas of the northeast, south, and west, lower SES children in a rural area, and middle SES children in an eastern city. At all of the sites the children were divided into groups of viewers and nonviewers in nursery school and viewers and nonviewers at home (1,124 children in all). The attempt was made to provide a familiar environment for testing with a relatively short test duration. The general technique consisted of three steps. A picture of an object was shown to the child. It was described, and the child was asked to respond (usually by pointing) to a question about the picture or object. (The tests had previously undergone an extensive period of development.) Measurements included children's pretest and posttests, parents' questionnaires, viewing records, observation records, content analysis of the program, parent-teacher guide interviews, and teacher questionnaires.

Results of the first year's evaluation may be summarized as follows:

1. Viewers learned more during the progress of the program series than did nonviewers; specifically, gains were observed in letters, numbers, and forms, as well as in the skills of sorting and classifying.

2. Consistent viewers learned far more than occasional viewers, with home viewers suffering no disadvantage in comparison with nursery school viewers.

3. There was no difference in gains between boys and girls after viewing the programs. Differences in gains for children from different social status were tied to prior achievement, which was mixed in turn with amount of viewing. There was also gain resulting from the mother's watching "Sesame Street" with the child and talking about the show with him. Children from Spanish-speaking homes who viewed consistently were the lowest group in pretest but the highest in posttest attainment, except for a relatively high-social-status rural group.

4. The greatest amount of visual attention was paid to Ernie, Gordon with the Muppets, Susan and Big Bird together, and visiting well-known stars. In all segments observed, girls seemed to have a slightly higher visual attention span than boys. Animals with or without accompanying people were of less visual interest than animals with Muppets. Songs and animation were the most well received of the production techniques, with books and films the least attractive. Lower-social-status children reacted more overtly—visually, verbally, and motorically—than middle-status children.

The results of the evaluation not only provided a basis for defining the success of the program, but were further useful in diagnosing the first year's effort. For example, the evaluation raised such concerns as whether the curriculum was a poor preparation for learning to read, whether the goals of the program were too narrowly conceived and thus more greatly assured success, whether the program was adequately oriented to the culture of Spanish-speaking children, and whether sequences that attempted rote learning could be improved.

Questions posed for the second-year evaluation were:
1. Can the findings of the first year be replicated? (The "New Study")
2. What are the effects of the revised sites and curriculum? (The "New Study")
3. Were the first year's effects cumulative? (The "Follow-up Study"—longitudinal)

The New Study concentrated mainly on at-home, urban, disadvantaged children, representing the main target population. Two new sites included children who had not seen "Sesame Street" during its first year. The Follow-up Study retained three disadvantaged urban sites. New items and tests were developed to assess the new goals; old items and tests were included to measure the effectiveness of goals on new viewers. Again, the study involved testing groups of children (283) who could be divided into viewer/nonviewer populations.

The results of the second-year evaluation for the New Study supported the first-year findings of goal effectiveness for disadvantaged preschool children. Goal effectiveness is described as impact on, rather than perfect mastery of, goal behaviors. The general results revealed that disadvantaged preschoolers continued to benefit from the show's emphasis on basic knowledge and skills, and older and more advantaged children benefited from the presentation of more complex knowledge and skills. In evaluating Spanish-background viewers it was not possible to replicate the unusually large gains made in the first year; results were inconclusive. Results of the Follow-up Study showed greatest effects in the cognitive domian. Since most of the first year's material was learned in the first year, it was deemed necessary to introduce new goal areas each year in order to have a continuing educational impact on children viewing the series for more than one year.

A further dividend of the evaluation of a series such as "Sesame Street" has been that it provides a basis for expanding the kinds of questions that may be raised about the effects of educational programming for children, as well as making such questions more precise. For example, the concern with reading skills led to "The Electric Company," a new series that is devoted entirely to developing such skills. In teaching basic reading skills to the seven- to-ten-year-old age group, the objectives could be specifically defined within such skills as decoding words, spelling, and basic sight vocabulary.[2]

Another question raised in the evaluation of "Sesame Street" was the effect of the viewing environment upon learning gains. Children who view the program and have the opportunity to interact with their

5

mothers about it have greater gains than children who simply view the program. The child seems to become a more active educational participant if circumstances prompt him to use items learned from the program, such as the use of special toys or some type of interchange with parents or peers. A more general question is raised of how, with any type of educational series, supplementary activities may be encouraged. This may be done either by schools, viewing groups, parents, or educational materials available to the student.

One further important question raised in the evaluation of "Sesam Street" was the influence of the program on the affective domain, as in personality development and social behavior, as well as attitudes about what may have been learned cognitively.

THE CHALLENGE OF "CARRASCOLENDAS"

The United States has the seventh largest Spanish-speaking population in the world. Of some 10 million Spanish speakers in the United States, approximately 92 percent are Mexican-Americans, and of this percentage over half are concentrated in the states of Texas, New Mexico, California, Colorado, and Arizona. A significant number of children found within this population come from homes where Spanish is the primary language. Although they have been exposed to English, many of these children do not have sufficient mastery of it to benefit fully from English instruction in the primary grades. This is the main argument for the need for bilingual education. That is, Spanish should be used to the extent that it will lessen the linguistic barrier in the classroom.

According to the U.S. Commission on Civil Rights, approximately three out of five Mexican-American children in Texas cannot speak English as well as their Anglo classmates.[3] It is these children who are the target of typical bilingual education programs. Bilingual education for these children does not mean Spanish only; it means the concurrent use of Spanish and English as the language of instruction. While lessening the barriers to education, such programs provide the basis for the child to develop as a bilingual in English and Spanish. Contrary to popular myth, there are no scientific grounds for believing that a child's developing two languages, rather than one, is any handicap. Programs of bilingual education are in direct contrast to the practices of monolingual instruction in English with minority-group children where the use of the second language was not only discouraged but was often "outlawed" with a threat of punishment.

Although the primary reason for bilingual education is a more practical one—to teach the child in a language that he can understand—there are other important reasons for such instruction. In the domain of personality and affective development of the child, bilingual instruction appears to lessen the child's anxiety and negative image of himself. Such instruction implies that bilingualism is "all right" and that there are a number of assets in being bilingual. Various experts point out that effective bilingual education also becomes bicultural education.[4]

People who are functionally bilingual often operate daily in two cultures. Thus at least some of the Spanish language used in bilingual education with Mexican-American children should be tied to cultural concepts and ideas reflecting the Mexican-American heritage. The bicultural attitude in bilingual education lessens the chance that the use of Spanish would be only a kind of sterile translation of English. The child who is functionally bilingual does not typically use one language as a direct translation of another. There are, however, many examples of interference and colloquialisms; for example:

I'll call you back. (Colloquial usage: Te llamo para atrás.) (Preferred: Te vuelvo a llamar.)

We'll pick you up after school. (Colloquial usage: Te levantamos después de la escuela.) (Preferred: Te recogemos después de las clases.)

It is important for the child not only to see the contrasts between English and Spanish linguistically, but also functionally in terms of usage in their subcultures. This bilingual/bicultural approach to education also gives the child a sense of worth about himself and his heritage. It allows him to see things from more than one point of view. It develops his ability to see how one's culture, attitudes, and ideas are not really "better" than someone else's, but simply different. In a broad sense, bilingual/bicultural education engenders the attitudes of cultural pluralism at the expense of ethnocentrism.

The greatest impetus for the development of programs of bilingual education in the United States came from the passage of the Title VII programs in the National Defense and Education Act of 1967. As part of an omnibus series of education bills, Title VII, The Bilingual Education Act, has the goal of meeting the special educational needs of children (1) whose ability to speak English is limited, (2) whose dominant language in the home environment is not English, and (3) who are from low-income families.

When implemented, Title VII programs provide funds and guidance for schools to develop bilingual classrooms. This includes the development of instructional materials, the training of teachers, and the formal evaluation of the bilingual classrooms as compared to traditional ones. By 1972, approximately one-fourth of the schools in Arizona, California, Colorado, New Mexico, and Texas had bilingual education classes in Spanish.

"Carrascolendas" was initiated in July 1970 as a special bilingual program project.[5] The content of "Carrascolendas" was initially

7

designed to reinforce and supplement existing classroom bilingual instructional programs while taking advantage of the unique opportunities offered by the television medium. The series incorporated a broad range of presentational techniques such as actors, puppets, films, music, dance, and special effects to provide innovative, attractive, and entertaining enrichment of classroom activities. In the development of program material, emphasis was placed on bilingualism, Mexican-American culture, the Mexican and Spanish heritage, and the multicultural society of the United States. Throughout the series the Spanish language, Mexican-American actors, Mexican-American personalities, music, games, dances, rhymes, and other elements of Hispanic tradition reflected the bilingual/bicultural environment of the target audience.

Consonant with the aims of the existing bilingual education programs and classrooms, the primary goal of "Carrascolendas" was to facilitate the children's knowledge gains in selected first- and second-grade content areas, and to increase their usage skills in both the English and Spanish languages. "Carrascolendas" was also planned as a public broadcast series that could supplement programs like "Sesame Street" for Mexican-American children. The behavioral objectives for the first-year series were developed within five broad knowledge categories. In each of these categories, some of the objectives were carried out exclusively in Spanish, and others exclusively in English. The following capsule descriptions illustrate these categories with different examples in English and Spanish:

1. Multicultural Social Environment—knowing why it is good to speak both Spanish and English; talking about family and relatives using English and Spanish vocabulary.

¿Es tu familia como esta?

Is it good to know how to speak English and Spanish? Why?

2. Language Skills—knowing certain vocabulary, syntax, and sound features of Spanish and English.

¿A quién les hablamos cuando hay una quemazón?

Whose shoes are those?

3. Numbers and Figures—counting; picking out pairs, sets of threes; recognizing numbers and figures.

Dame la letra que tiene el sonido /o/.

Put a circle around the sets of threes.

4. Physical Environment—recognizing certain items in the immediate environment, names of animals, of foods, and transportation items.

¿Qué es esto? (elefante)

Do you know where bread comes from? Where?

5. Concept Development—recognizing size and differences, causes of hot and cold, and weight differences.

8

¿Eres tú más chico que tu papá? ¿Cuándo lo vas a alcanzar? What do you wear so you don't get cold?

Based upon behavioral objectives, a series of 30 half-hour programs was developed in the first year of the project. Individual programs were comprised of segments originally ranging from twenty seconds to five minutes. Each of these segments was developed to carry out a specific behavioral objective or multiple objectives. An attempt was made to balance the English- and Spanish-language segments within each program.

The setting for the series is Carrascolendas, a mythical town in South Texas inhabited by the program's principal figures. In the first year these were "Señorita Barrera" and "Señor Villarreal" who often provided introductory and closing materials for each program. Other characters included "Agapito," a mischievous lion; "Marieta," a young girl; "Don Pedro," a house painter; and "Mr. Jones," the owner of a hamburger stand. All of these characters, with the exception of Mr. Jones, played in both English and Spanish segments. This cast was regularly augmented by two bilingual puppets, "Ruperto" and "Manolín." In addition to these principal figures, other personalities appeared once or twice during the series; included among these were prominent Mexican-Americans from the Central Texas area who appeared in cameo roles.

A typical program included the following:

1. a brief skit in which Marieta is attempting to teach Agapito how to make tortillas, emphasizing the fact that they must be round;

2. a direct instructional segment, where Don Pedro pronounces a Spanish vowel in isolation and then, with the use of picture cards, gives examples of names of objects that begin with that vowel;

3. a children's song, usually in Spanish, set into the context of a skit involving the principal characters; and

4. a puppet sequence where Ruperto and Manolín attempt to share the same umbrella. Interspersed between these segments might be direct drills on letters or numbers similar to the "Sesame Street" commercials. Some segments were repeated within the same program. The program, created for a bicultural audience, was itself markedly bilingual and bicultural. The first year's series was produced in the fall and winter of 1970 and was regionally broadcast initially from February through April of 1971.

The format for the second-year program series of "Carrascolendas" was similar to the first, except for a number of innovations based upon experience in the first year. Although some behavioral objectives were carried over from the first series, categories were revised along the following lines:

1. Self-concept—knowing about one's self, recognizing cultural heritage, and knowing suitable ways to express emotions.

¿Qué idiomas hablas?

Name someone, a person or an animal, who needs you to help him.

2. Science—skills such as identifying life cycles of certain animals, knowing processes such as making bread, and being able to identify environmental sights and sounds.

¿Cuál se rompe facilmente? (piedra, madera, hierro, vidrio)

Put these pictures in order to show how honey is made.

3. History/Culture—knowing legends, songs, and facts of Texas and Mexican history.

¿Cómo se le dice a las cáscaras de huevo que tienen confetti?

What are piñatas used for? (visual: a piñata)

4. Language Skills—knowing certain words in Spanish and English, selected syntactic patterns, and sound contrasts in Spanish and English.

¿Cómo se le dice a la persona que hace pan?

This is a picture of a mouse. In this picture there are two of them. There are two_____. (visual: 2 mice)

5. Phoneme/Grapheme Relations—knowing relationships between sounds and their corresponding letters, as a skill relevant to reading.

¿Cuál de estas letras es la /k/? (qu, x, z, r, b)

6. Math—learning certain sets, counting, and symbol recognition.

¿Qué hora es? (reloj: 3:00)

Color one-third of this ball. (sheet: ball divided into thirds)

Some of the distinguishing characteristics of the second-year series included the use of color and additional production techniques. Animation was one of the most successful and frequently used of these. A larger cast and more elaborate costuming supplemented that of the previous year. The original format included Spanish-speaking hand puppets; in the second year English-speaking hand puppets and English-speaking actors portraying marionettes were added. (All the hand puppets were eliminated in the third year.) A "concentration board" and "reading machine" were new developments in the second year of the series.*

Dramatic segments and films were lengthened. Sometimes the same film was shown twice in one program, once in Spanish and once in English. This differed somewhat from the method of film presentation used in the first year, when two different films were sometimes shown in one program, or one film was shown in English or in Spanish.

_____

*The concentration board is composed of 49 blank squares that flip to reveal drawings, letters, or numbers. The reading machine presented letter, syllable, word, and sentence formation in Spanish on a large television-like machine illustrating both the sentence presented and a scene representing the sentence.

The second year's series was produced late in the fall and winter of 1971 and broadcast from February through April of 1972. The initial version of the second year's series was broadcast regionally and evaluated only in Texas.

During the summer of 1972 the second year's series was reedited and eventually broadcast nationally from October through December of 1972. The Spanish narration of films and the reading machine segments were eliminated. Dance segments were added to the program, along with additional cameo or guest appearances. Presentations of songs were introduced and supplemented by dramatized drills.*

To facilitate classroom use of "Carrascolendas," a package of supplementary materials was developed each year and distributed as a Teacher Guide. The Guide contained activities and songs coordinated with television segments of "Carrascolendas," as well as additional activities not tied to the program. In the first year the Guide was compiled in a looseleaf notebook format containing visual-aid sheets. This was replaced in the second year by a permanent, bound book, plus a visuals kit. The second year's book was organized according to activities for specific skill areas, as well as program-by-program. The third year's Guide was very similar to the second, except that the results of an evaluation carried out in the second year were used as a basis for some revision and editing.

The evaluations designed for "Carrascolendas" focused on assessment of the effects of the series, primarily measured by pupils' learning gains on behavioral objectives, and secondarily measured by surveys of teachers' evaluations and attitudes toward the program. In the terminology of educational research, these were product evaluations done in a summative manner. The evaluators also participated in formative evaluations that included working with the educational planners and television producer on the initial evaluation of the behavioral objectives selected for the program. Evaluation activities further included a number of related studies, particularly in the second and third years of the project. Finally, the research team participated in a process evaluation for each year of the project. These evaluations were meant to assess the overall management organization of the project, the degree to which this organization functioned according to predetermined goals and schedule, and the development of suggestions for increasing the efficiency of the management process.

---

*A still newer series was produced in 1972-73. It retained the same format developed during 1971-72 and eliminated all hand puppets. These 30 additional programs were broadcast nationally by the Public Broadcasting Service in the fall of 1973.

NOTES

1. For a detailed description of overall evaluations of the first and second years of "Sesame Street," see Samuel Ball and Gerry Ann Bogatz, The First Year of Sesame Street: An Evaluation (Princeton, N.J.: Educational Testing Service, October 1970), and Gerry Ann Bogatz and Samuel Ball, The Second Year of Sesame Street: A Continuing Evaluation (Princeton, N.J.: Educational Testing Service, November 1971).

2. Samuel Ball and Gerry Ann Bogatz, Reading with Television: An Evaluation of The Electric Company, Vol. 1 (Princeton, N.J.: Educational Testing Service, February 1973).

3. U.S. Commission on Civil Rights, Report V: Mexican-American Educational Study, "Differences in Teacher Interaction with Mexican-American and Anglo Students" (Washington, D.C.: U.S. Government Printing Office, March 1973).

4. For further elaboration of these points, see Manuel Reyes Mazon, ed., Adelante: An Emerging Design for Mexican-American Education (New York: Appleton-Century-Crofts, forthcoming).

5. The idea for this series was initially conceived by Aida Barrera of The University of Texas Communication Center (station KLRN). Ms. Barrera eventually became executive producer of the series. Title VII programs can only be funded with schools or education agencies; the primary contract for the series was developed through the Education Service Center, Region XIII, at Austin, Texas. Region XIII, as the primary contractor, subcontracted to KLRN for the development of the series and to the Center for Communication Research at The University of Texas for its evaluation. Michael Pool of the Education Service Center served as the project coordinator along with Ms. Carol Perkins, developer of the curriculum materials.

2

CREATING
"CARRASCOLENDAS"

PROJECT ORGANIZATION

"Carrascolendas" was originally organized as a special bilingual education project, supported under Title VII funds. The principal contractor was the Education Service Center (Region XIII), which subcontracted the production of the series through station KLRN at The University of Texas. The Education Service Center provided a curriculum staff, comprised of a "television coordinator," who administered the overall project, and a "curriculum coordinator," who was in charge of developing behavioral objectives. The Regional Service Center was also responsible for letting a contract to an independent evaluation agency each year and this was the affiliation of the Center for Communication Research at The University of Texas. An "executive producer" with KLRN was responsible for all aspects of design and coordination of production of the series, including such further administrative tasks as distribution of the series, certain aspects of publicity, and fiscal operations of the production component. A further component in the organization was an advisory committee, comprised primarily of local persons with an interest or expertise in bilingual education (including parents), who would counsel both the television coordinator and the executive producer in the formulation, critique, and evolution of the program series. Finally, the evaluation component was charged with carrying out a formal field assessment of the project to determine the degree to which it met its intended objectives.

The operation and interrelation of these units can be summarized as follows:

1. The television coordinator and curriculum coordinator prepared descriptions of behavioral objectives of the program and suggested content for the communication of those objectives.

2. The executive producer and staff reviewed the objectives and content materials provided by the television coordinator and then prepared drafts of program scripts.

3. Program scripts were reviewed for suitability in terms of educational objectives by the television coordinator and his staff, delegates of the advisory committee, and members of the evaluation team.

4. Given revised program scripts, production was begun on segments.

5. The television coordinator and his staff prepared a Teacher Guide to be sent to schools that would use the series. This staff also handled dissemination and publicity of the series.

6. The research team conducted field evaluations of the series.

Although the above steps are accurate, it would be misleading to say that they were followed exactly or even that they worked with the best of efficiency. To provide some idea of problems that arose in the management of a project and how these were sometimes eliminated, we have included a summary of management evaluations in Chapter 8, which was a further duty of the evaluation team.

ORIGIN OF THE PROGRAM

It is important to recognize that underlying the detailed and precisely defined educational objectives of the series there were decisions about the much more subjective and creative content that was used to communicate those objectives. Accordingly, most of the creative aspects of "Carrascolendas" are found not in the detailed educational objectives but in the content developed for the most part by the series' executive producer, Aida Barrera.

Ms. Barrera attributes the idea for the bilingual television series to experiences growing out of televised language programs that she had been producing for several years for station KLRN. In the course of developing programs for teaching Spanish to English speakers, she was often impressed with the effectiveness of short, fast-moving segments that attempted to teach a point about language in the context of an entertaining scene, as in the behavior of a puppet, or anything that was functional and highly interesting. She had also noted that the more realistic the language included in the scenes, the more such segments also communicated something of the cultural context of the language. These kinds of segments—with a single objective or two, highly interesting, and often including a "character"—seemed to benefit from the personalized and intense focus offered by the television medium. Evidence of the potential of this approach with young children was also provided by the success of "Sesame Street." This made the development of a bilingual children's television series all the more attractive.

Ms. Barrera, a Mexican-American bilingual from South Texas, was particularly sensitive to the educational problems of the Mexican-American child. In a special television segment developed to introduce the program to teachers, she summarized the problem as follows:

> Teachers tell us that many of our children have lost a sense of self-identity and self-concept. Many are overly inhibited. They have retreated within themselves because they simply cannot relate to what they see around them. There is something wrong, they think, with people who speak Spanish. There is something wrong with being a Mexican-American. That which is a part of them and which should rightfully be a source of pride has all too often become a source of shame. And so they look down at the floor and do not talk.[1]

This kind of problem, in Ms. Barrera's terms, has served as the mainspring for the overall goals for the series:

> If we were to choose a single goal for the series, we would say that what we are trying to do through "Carrascolendas" is to change attitudes. We want to change people's attitudes about the Mexican-American child. But most important, we want to insure that the Mexican-American child's attitude about himself is positive and confident.[2]

In creating the content for "Carrascolendas," Ms. Barrera has drawn heavily from her own bilingual and bicultural experiences for ideas on content. Her strategy has been to create segments in which Spanish is used as it is in everyday life. Many of these situations have been recalled from her own experiences.

> We present Spanish as a language that is natural and acceptable. Because television is essentially a dramatic medium, we rely heavily on dramatic techniques to get our point across. We cannot duplicate the child's exact environment, but we can permeate our presentations with those things which are unique to the Spanish speaking culture. We involve the children in situations dealing with foods, customs, jokes, jingles, sayings, and life styles that are familiar to Mexican-Americans and to many other Spanish speakers. . . .

15

Our format is essentially a dramatic one. We try to play up the comical aspects and we try to do it in a picaresque fashion. We feel the picaresque is especially appropriate, because the roots of this dramatic form are Spanish-speaking ones.

We Spanish speakers love the pícaro and that is why this type is so common in our literature, our films, our television programs. Lazarillo, Cantinflas, Tin Tan, and Cachirulo are all antiheroes who live on the fringes of society and who survive by their wits. They are marginal, negative beings who have no pretense about themselves and who are not taken in by the pretenses of others.

I grew up watching Mexican-American comedies—as a matter of fact, my job when I was 13 years old was selling candy and popcorn at a Mexican theater in South Texas. (I am afraid I ate more candy than I sold.) We delighted in watching the ragamuffin pícaro outwit them all. Somehow the pícaro with his silly jokes and his ragged clothes held out a hope for us. Somehow he told us, if I can do it, so can you. That's the sort of feeling we want to convey in "Carrascolendas." That's the sort of thing we want our characters, Agapito, Tacho, Nacho, and Juana, to tell our children. We want them to hold out a hope. We want them to say, perhaps not explicitly, but implicitly, if we can do it, so can you.

But why the name "Carrascolendas?" And what does "Carrascolendas" mean? Again, at the risk of sounding too personal, I'll tell you why the name was chosen. I was born in a small Texas town whose original name was Carnestolendas. Carnestolendas is an authentic Spanish name which means carnival. Soon after the founding of the town the name was changed, but the townspeople delighted in remembering their origins and verbally transmitted the name from one generation to another. The verbal transmission got confused and soon the name "Carrascolendas" was being used. The new name had acquired an authenticity of its own, the authenticity given to it by the Mexican-American community that had wrought the change. We felt that for a number of reasons "Carrascolendas" was an appropriate name for a mythical television town. First of all it had a fanciful ring that we felt would appeal to a child's imagination. And second, but more important, was that in a sense, it was truly a product of the Mexican-American situation. "Carrascolendas" shows us that language is a thing that is alive.

16

It clearly indicates that both language and its accompanying culture root their authenticity in this very fact. We like "Carrascolendas" because it is truly a part of us.[3]

PROGRAM FORMAT

During each of its first three years of production, "Carrascolendas" was a 30-program series of half-hour shows. The format is a variety of segments, some running only a few seconds, others up to four or five minutes. Continuity is provided in the setting for most of these segments, the imaginary town of "Carrascolendas", and in the four or five main characters who appear in each year's series. The character who has been maintained throughout the series is a bilingual lion named Agapito. Agapito is big, somewhat clumsy, very outgoing, and always willing to learn something new, although his learning sometimes has its problems.

The accompanying pictures present some of the characters who have appeared in the series since production was initially begun in 1970.

SEGMENT DESIGN

In the first year of the series, the dramatic segments and the films were typically four or five minutes long. Based upon experiences from the first year's evaluation, most segments are now reduced to three or fewer minutes. No attempt is made to introduce a particular segment or to have special transition material between segments. However, when segments are combined for a 30-minute program, considerable attention is given to the "flow" from one segment to another, to variety in types of segments, and to the inclusion of logically ordered behavioral objectives.

"Carrascolendas" uses almost equal amounts of Spanish and English, but any one collection of segments in the 30-minute program may be weighted slightly in one direction or the other. During the first year's series, films were four to six minutes long and narrated either in Spanish or English. In the second year, films were shortened to three minutes and were repeated in a single program, first giving the narration in English, and then in Spanish. In the reedited version aired during the third year, films were shown only once per program, always in English and usually within the first ten minutes of the program. The Spanish segments, by contrast, are usually shorter than the English ones; they often consist of rhymes, riddles, games, and jokes. Every program begins with a song or an animated sequence,

17

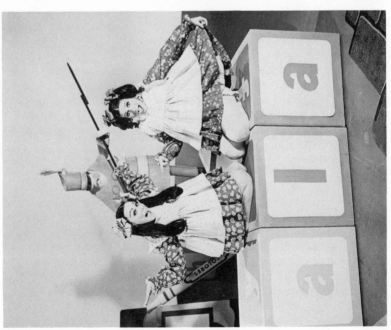

18

21

which have been found in our evaluation to be the two most popular aspects of the program. The format for Program 19 (1972) provides examples of the duration of each segment, the language used, and the order of the segments.

Time		Segment	Language
0:47	1.	Intro	
0:30	2.	Filler: Dance Freeze #8	Spanish
0:21	3.	Math: Disappearing Balloons	Spanish
0:41	4.	Animation:/gw/ GÜ	Spanish
1:44	5.	Song: "The World Is Round" (REPEAT)	English
2:59	6.	Film: The Truck	English
0:20	7.	Filler: Adult Cameo #1	Spanish
0:19	8.	Cameos: /gw/ GÜ	Spanish
0:30	9.	Filler: Dance Freeze #5	Spanish
1:27	10.	Song: "Stand, Everybody, Side by Side" (REPEAT)	English
3:58	11.	Dramatic: The Falling Ball	Spanish
1:01	12.	Animation:/g/ G (REPEAT)	Spanish
0:30	13.	Filler: Dance Freeze #11	Spanish
2:17	14.	Puppets: Willy and Gravity	English
1:31	15.	Song: "Naricita, Naricita"	Spanish
0:33	16.	Math: Subtracting Lights	Spanish
0:27	17.	Filler: Adult Cameo #4—La Navaja (The Knife)	Spanish
1:01	18.	Animation /g/ GU (REPEAT)	Spanish
1:18	19.	Dramatic: In/On	English
1:44	20.	Song: "La Vieja Inés" (REPEAT)	Spanish
0:14	21.	Math: Disappearing Balloons	Spanish
0:30	22.	Filler: Dance Freeze #13	Spanish
0:41	23.	Animation: /gw/ GÜ (REPEAT)	Spanish
2:07	24.	Song: "B and V" (REPEAT)	English
0:30	25.	Filler: Dance Freeze #9	Spanish
0:20	26.	Close	
28:20			

Like any television script, the script for "Carrascolendas" includes descriptions of characterization, sets, music, props, and the like. But beyond this, each script contains descriptions of the behavioral objectives for each segment, so that the production staff and the performers are aware of the educational aims underlying what they are preparing. The following script example is for a dramatic segment in Spanish in Program 19 of the second-year series. Agapito and Tina learn about the force of gravity from Sr. Villarreal.

Sample Script

Program 19

OBJECTIVES: The child knows that gravity has "pull."
The child can demonstrate that gravity has pull and
he can measure it. (He hangs a book on an elastic
band tied to a door handle and shows how much the
elastic has stretched.)

Language: Spanish
Characters: Agapito
Tina
Sr. Villarreal
Setting: Multilevel Set
Visuals: None
Props: 2 balls
Book
Clothes hanger
Large rubber band
Costumes: Characters' outfits
Music: Arranger's choice

(Tina enters with one ball, throws it up. Ball falls. She tries
again and the same thing occurs. She looks puzzled. Agapito
enters.)

Ti: Esta vez sí se queda arriba.

(Tina repeats action.)

Ti: Esta vez, sí se queda arriba.

(Tina repeats action.)

Ag: Déjame a mí. Hmmm. (Does same with ball.)
No se quiere quedar arriba.

(Both repeat action with two balls. Sr. Villarreal comes in,
observes their action, follows movement with head. . .puzzled
look. . .)

Ti: Mire, Sr. Villarreal. . .aventamos esta pelota hacia
arriba. . .

Ag: Y siempre se cae al suelo. . .

Sr.V: Claro.

Ti: ¿Por qué no se queda arriba?

Sr.V: Pues. . .porque no.

Ag: Pero. . .¿por qué no?

Sr.V: Pues. . .se trata de la fuerza de gravedad.

Ti: ¿Qué. . .qué?

Sr.V: Se trata de la fuerza de gravedad.

Ti: Agapito. . .se trata de la fuerza de gravedad.

Ag: Ah, se trata de la fuerza de gravedad. Claro.

23

(Agapito and Tina sort of look at each other, then at Sr. Villarreal, then at each other.)

Ti: Oye, Agapito. . .¿sabes qué quiere decir eso de la fuerza de gravedad?

Ag: Pues, mira Tina. . .te digo la verdad. . .este. . . nooooo. . .

Sr.V: Miren, déjenme enseñarles. (Demonstrates with book, clothes hanger and elastic.) ¿Ven este libro? . . .voy a tomarlo y le voy a poner un elastico. . .así. . .ahora lo voy a colgar de este gancho. . . Miren lo que pasa. . fíjense cómo el elástico se pone muy tirante. Ahora. . ¿por qué ocurre eso?

Ti: Pues quién sabe. . .

Ag: No sé. . .

Sr.V: Por la fuerza de gravedad. La fuerza de la tierra atrae el libro. . .y estira el elástico. A ver, mira, Tina acuéstate en el suelo. Tu eres la tierra. Ahora di "libro, ven hacia mí." (Sr. Villarreal will get on higher level so that he will place dangling book above Tina. Tina flat on the floor will repeat sentence as the book dangles towards her.)

Ti: Libro, ven hacia mí. Libro, ven hacia mí.

Sr.V: ¿Ves, Agapito? Tina es la tierra. . .y ¿ves cómo la tierra está atrayendo el libro? Ahora, sigan jugando . . .que me tengo que ir.

Ag & Ti: Adiós, Sr. Villarreal.

(Tina is still lying on the floor. Agapito will attempt to step on her. Yell from Tina.)

Ti: Ay. . .fíjate por dónde pisas.

Ag: Yo (looking around) . . . yo sólo estoy pisando sobre la tierra. (Looking down) . . . Aquí no veo mas que tierra. (Holding foot over Tina) . . . y la tierra está atrayendo mi pie. (Camera shot over foot and Tina's head.) (Loud yell and smothered sound from Tina.)

Ti: Ayyyyy. Ayyyyyy.

Ag: Shhh. . .tierra, no hagas tanto ruido. Te va a oír la gente.

Short of having the reader view the program first hand, the best way to appreciate the flavor and pace of the program is to read a description of the series of segments that made up one of the actual programs. A viewer's impressions of the program of which the foregoing script is a part, follow.

Gay music, peppy and rhythmic, accompanies the introductory animated title sequence in which parts of the name "Carrascolendas" are arranged on the television screen. Then, in a boisterous half-minute dance hall scene, the dancers freeze while one couple presents a riddle in Spanish.

The next segment, even briefer, and also in Spanish, shows Pirulín, Agapito the lion, and four big colorful balloons. Agapito delightedly pops them one by one to illustrate the mathematical concept of zero.

A quick animation segment in Spanish presents the words cigüeña and paragüitas. A stork appears; it starts to rain and he tries to protect himself with a very tiny umbrella. The key words are repeated, slowly and clearly.

The English song, "The World Is Round," is introduced by a film of a rocket launch. A large globe of the earth is spun, while Agapito teaches the "man from outer space" the science concepts of rotation and revolution around the sun causing day and night.

The second longest segment of the program is the English film, The Truck, narrated by Tito the truck. The truck gets fuel, has its engine adjusted, and carefully pulls out onto the highway, crossing a bridge and overpass on its way.

The film is followed by a 20-second cameo in which Cuca asks a rhyming riddle in Spanish. She tries to put the riddle's answer, a ring, on the finger of Herman the marionette. Though there is much effort expended in pushing and shoving, the ring is still too small for his finger.

Two quick cameos in Spanish present the "gü" sound, and its written form in the words güera and cigüeña. We see the film of a lovely, blond little girl (güera) named Guillermina, and a stork (cigüeña).

A dance freeze, again in the dance hall atmosphere, is used as background for a different Spanish rhyme. This is followed by the English song, "Stand, Everybody, Side by Side." The music throughout is rhythmic and sprightly.

A dramatic sketch in Spanish, the longest segment on this program, has Agapito, Tina, and Sr. Villarreal demonstrate the pull of gravity. Sr. Villarreal is able to clarify the puzzled queries of the others about why the balls they are tossing in the air always come back down again. The results of teaching this science concept are humorous and effective, especially when Tina lies on the floor to portray the earth and Agapito teasingly dangles his huge foot above her face to show how the pull of gravity brings his paw down closer and closer. This scene ends when Agapito tosses a ball again and looks with amazement when it fails to come down (on camera, that is).

An animated Spanish segment presenting the sound and written letter g shows a rooster (gallo) eating a worm (gusano) and becoming extremely fat (gordo) as a result.

Another quick dance freeze and riddle are presented.

The puppets, Willy and Sam, repeat the content of the science objective in an English scene in which Sam enlightens Willy about the pull of gravity.

The Spanish song "Naricita, Naricita" ("little nose") is sung by Pete to a big dog with a huge nose.

Herman narrates the math concept of zero by showing how the four windows of a doll house are darkened, one by one, until all the lights are out.

In a brief cameo Agapito says a riddle in Spanish, while Milly, dressed like a carpenter, tries to open her pocket knife which is the answer to the riddle. She is unable to do so and finally gives up in frustration, trying to cut wood with the closed knife.

A puppet stage, a soldier puppet, and a guitar are animated presentations of guiñol, guerrero and guitarra which present the grapheme gu with the phoneme /g/.

An English dramatic segment illustrating the prepositions "on" and "in" is portrayed by the Professor, Herman, Agapito, Pirulín, Srta. Barrera, Sr. Villarreal, and the children. Large cutouts of a train, bus, and car fancifully "drive" the point home. The children interact with lively enthusiasm as a kind of Greek chorus.

The Spanish song, "La Vieja Inés," is done brightly by several characters seated around the kitchen table. They delve into a large fruit bowl for the pieces of fruit appropriate for each verse of this song about colors.

Agapito makes some balloons disappear again to illustrate the subtraction fact: $5 - 2 = 3$.

Agapito has a humorous answer to the Spanish riddle Tina asks him in the dance freeze. This is followed by a repetition of the stork animation presented earlier in the program.

Most of the show's characters, with the help of ten children, sing the English "B/V Song." The viewer is encouraged to repeat the contrasting pairs of words: bat/vat, boat/vote, and best/vest.

The show ends with a final dance freeze in which Pete asks Cuca another funny riddle.

DEVELOPMENT OF PRODUCTION STRATEGIES

One mark of the production strategies of "Carrascolendas" has been an evolution from year to year in the selection and implementatio of various techniques. Some of these, according to the executive

TABLE 2.1

"CARRASCOLENDAS" Production Staff Organization

POSITION	ROLE DELINEATION
Executive Producer*	Administrative director of the project, hires personnel, supervises production, approves all materials used in the series, supervises and prepares scripts, serves as Project official representative.
Producer*	Coordinates and supervises personnel, critiques scripts, supervises and approves taping sessions and props, records audio promotions and Spanish narrations, determines repetition sequencing of segments.
Bilingual Curriculum Specialist*	Evaluates curriculum materials for need and appropriateness, suggests specific curricula for meeting objectives, serves as resource person, coordinates children's activities, arranges and schedules film trips, schedules publicity sessions.
Supervising Director of Production	Supervises production and editing of the series, maintains color production standards, coordinates activities of producer-director-design groups, consults with film producer regarding film segments, supervises music and audio mixes, special effects, and dubbing.
Spanish Language Consultant	Critiques, approves, or revises all Spanish segments, assists in writing of correspondence and legal documents in Spanish, provides information on cultural studies and language pertinent to the Mexican-American child in the United States.
Director of Segments	Directs all studio-produced segments, supervises audio recording sessions, assists in video-tape editing, coordinates requests for, and shipping of, sample programs to interested persons or organizations.
Musical Director	Composes original music for programs, screens and selects other original compositions, researches and locates music reflective of Mexican culture, negotiates licenses for copyrighted music, hires, rehearses, and conducts all music sessions.

(continued)

27

TABLE 2.1, continued

POSITION	ROLE DELINEATION
Designer	Designs and constructs sets and additional art materials, puppets, animal characters, and special effects, designs and implements animation elements, designs and produces art for brochures and fliers.
Assistant Producer*	Researches folkloric and educational materials, procures all stage properties for rehearsals and taping sessions, consults with other personnel regarding design and staging concept of each segment.
Assistant Producer, Staging*	Attends all taping sessions, assists in blocking and rehearsing segments for production, assists Costume and Scene Designers in procuring production properties.
Costume Designer and Costumer	Designs and constructs or procures costumes for all segments, collaborates with make-up artist and actors to facilitate use of costumes for dramatic purposes.
Engineer	Records all segments, orders and evaluates all videotapes, coordinates activities of other technical personnel, advises production staff, maintains equipment, and oversees recording and shipment of videotape dubs.
Assistant Director and Videotape Editor	Assists Supervising Director and Director of Segments, arranges for dubbing and shipment of preview tapes, provides special audio effects, edits taped program materials into finished segments, adds necessary postproduction materials when editing.
Production Assistants*	Assist with production, staging activities, and office procedures.
Additional Staff	Part-time actors.

*These people combine regular duties with acting and are regular characters appearing in the series.

28

producer and her staff, are closely tied to the financial resources available to the program. When funds were available, they were used for more elaborate sets, professional performers, copyrighted music, and animation. Although the production budget did not increase substantially over the three years, there was some increase in funds each year. One main change over the years of production was to center upon fewer objectives each year. Four or five instructional objectives were squeezed into many of the segments during the first-year series; an average of slightly over one instructional objective per segment was included in the third-year series. This coordinates with the decision to employ shorter segments after the evaluation of the first-year series.

Another trend was to increase the use of scenes that were either composed of close-up shots or did not involve more than a few people at a time. Field observation in schools indicated that often as many as 100 children viewed the program on a single television set, thus making it virtually impossible for the children to make much sense out of a scene that would include a large number of people or objects. It was found that printed or written material shown on the screen had to be exceptionally large in order to be seen by the viewing audience. The revised strategy was to use more close-ups in the series and to precede group scenes by close-ups, to help the child recognize characters and understand content.

Over the three-year period, the number of people employed on the production staff was based mostly on fiscal considerations, as well as the availability of qualified personnel. The core of the current staff includes 20 people, whose titles and general duties are described in Table 2.1. The hallmark of the staff organization operation of "Carrascolendas" is that most of the people are assigned to multiple duties.

NOTES

1. Taken from the script of the "Carrascolendas" pilot, Sept. 1973.
2. Ibid.
3. Ibid.

3

**EFFECTS ON
THE CHILDREN:
THE TEXAS STUDIES**

THE DESIGN OF FIELD EXPERIMENTS

The most detailed evaluation of the impact of the series on children was based on a series of field studies where certain children viewed the program and a comparable group did not. Subsequently, both groups of children were compared in terms of measures based upon the behavioral objectives of the program. Where viewer children had greater gains than nonviewers on these measures, the results could be interpreted as due to the program. Throughout the project, these studies are referred to as field experiments. In this chapter we summarize the experiments that were conducted over the three-year period in the state of Texas. In Chapter 4 we will describe the national study, which included experiments conducted in the third year outside the state of Texas.

Although field experiments are time consuming and costly, they offer the most objective way to determine the impact of the program. Since it is assumed that children will be learning some of the objectives of the program during their normal course of development quite apart from the effects of the program, it is important to be able to sort out such gains from those that can be attributed directly to the program. This is the main reason for testing groups of children who are comparable in every way except that one group has seen the program and the other has not. These groups are measured in terms of the behavioral objectives before and after viewing the entire program series. Every type of gain found for the children who viewed the program, above and beyond gains found for children who did not view, is a direct effect of viewing the series and not due just to the normal course of development. The results comprise the summative evaluation of the series.

To conduct experiments along these lines several assumptions are necessary:

1. that it is possible to specify in measurable terms the behaviors that are representative of the impact of the series;

2. that children can be sampled whose behavior can be interpreted as representative of the target audience of the series; and

3. that children who have viewed the program can be compared with a nonviewer group, allowing cause-effect conclusions to be drawn.

The types of measures used in our field experiments directly represented the intended effects of the program. Although we might expect the program to have a variety of general results, if it were to have any effect at all, we would expect to find within the children's behaviors evidence of the behavioral objectives that the program was designed to attain. Such a measurement approach involves the use of criterion-referenced testing. In simple terms, this means that test items are themselves a sampling of the behavioral objectives of the program. Thus, for example, we might specify that after hearing a brief story the child will know the names of at least three of the five animals in the story and be able to say those names in response to pictures of the animals. In the experiments conducted during the three years, the children were tested on groups of items taken from the behavioral objectives of the different content areas of the program.

One of the greatest challenges in conducting adequate measurement studies of young children is to employ a testing technique that maximizes a child's opportunity to provide a response. Put another way, the task is to eliminate conditions that might inhibit a child from responding. Inhibiting conditions loom large in the testing of minority-group children, particularly where class and ethnic differences between the tester and the child may cause the latter to be reticent. Also, it is difficult to use paper and pencil techniques with young children. Finally, there are problems in working with young children in groups where it is difficult to monitor individual performance.

In all experiments conducted in the "Carrascolendas" project, we employed a method of testing children individually in an oral interview situation. This approach is similar to methods of fieldwork undertaken in linguistic studies, particularly for data gathering with young children. The one-to-one interview situation makes it easy for the tester to monitor very closely the responses of the individual child and to insure that intervening conditions are not adversely affecting testing. Second, it is possible to develop an individual interview format that resembles conversational situations already familiar to the child. As much as possible, the people who did the fieldwork aided the teachers in the classrooms before the initial testing so that the children were quite familiar with them. This was particularly important in preparing the situation for the different language of the

31

interviews. Individuals who conducted the interviews in Spanish had identified themselves as Spanish speakers before testing the children, and similarly for English monolingual speakers. Consequently, when it came time for the children to be interviewed, most children already anticipated the language that the interviewer would use. Based upon the precautions just described, we would argue that the test data from all of these studies represented a maximum attempt to provide positive and consistent test conditions for the children.

The second assumption—sampling children representative of the target audience of the program—was difficult to satisfy adequately in the present studies because of the high cost of conducting experiments involving large numbers of children. In the first two years of the project, Mexican-American children in an Austin, Texas school were included in the experimental studies. In these first two years the programs were initially distributed in the state of Texas. Although we could not claim that the children in the test school were a representative sample of the total population of Mexican-American children, we could claim that if the program were to have impact, we should be able to observe it in these children. In the third year's design, when "Carrascolendas" was nationally distributed, funds were expanded to support evaluations in California, Arizona, New Mexico, Colorado, and Michigan, in addition to Texas. This greatly increased our ability to assess the effects of the program on different groups of Mexican-American children.

Comparing carefully matched viewer and nonviewer groups— the third assumption—was accomplished in the first two years of the project, when children in the test school were randomly divided into viewer and nonviewer groups. Every child had an equal chance of being in either group, and by such random assignment it could be assumed that the groups were generally equal. In the third year, due to the extensive range of test sites and diverse operating conditions, children were selected initially for viewer groups, then attempts were made to obtain smaller groups of children who were alike in every way except that they would not be in a viewer group. Methods of this selection varied somewhat, but for the most part the viewer and nonviewer groups were comparable. Finally, statistical procedures were employed to determine whether differences in average measures of viewer and nonviewer groups were greater than might be expected by chance alone. Such statistics were a basis for projecting the results beyond the sample of children actually tested.

The same type of research design was used in the experiments for each of the three years. Test instruments were developed to measure behavioral objectives in Spanish and in English. Groups of children selected to participate in the experiment were designated as viewers and nonviewers. Before viewing the series all children were given interview tests, separately in Spanish and English. They then viewed the series, which usually consisted of 30 half-hour programs broadcast three times a week. After viewing the series, both groups of children were given the same test materials. The test results of the viewer/nonviewer groups were compared to see whether there were differences favoring viewer groups. Any differences were interpreted as indicative of the effects of the program.

THE FIRST YEAR

Research Design

The first experiment was conducted between February and April of 1971 in Zavala Elementary School in Austin, Texas. Most of the children in the school came from Mexican-American families representing different degrees of bilingualism, urban or rural living experiences, economic levels, and political attitudes. Children from bilingual and traditional classrooms in first and second grades were randomly selected for assignment to viewer or nonviewer groups. It was possible, therefore, to compare viewers with nonviewers across first and second grades and across bilingual and traditional classrooms. Eighty-eight children were initially included in this study, 48 viewers and 40 nonviewers. Subdivisions by grades and type of classroom were approximately equal in size. All children in these samples were to some degree bilingual in Spanish and English. Within these groups, however, there was heterogeneity in terms of academic abilities, degrees of dominance in either the Spanish or English language, and the length of time that the family had lived in the city.

Separate interview formats were developed for Spanish and English. Each lasted approximately 35 minutes and represented a sampling of test items selected from among the behavioral objectives of the program. For the most part, items on the Spanish and English interview sequences for a given topical area (for example "multicultural social environment") were different. The test items represented a sampling from five broad "knowledge" categories of behavioral objectives described in Chapter 1. In each of these categories some of the objectives were carried out exclusively in Spanish and others exclusively in English. The categories, already described in Chapter 1, were multicultural social environment, language skills, numbers and figures, physical environment, and concept development.

Test scores were based on the number of items responded to correctly in each of the Spanish or the English test sequences. Within each language sequence there could be five subtest scores (for example, "multicultural social environment"). In most interpretations we converted the scores to percentages of correct answers. A child's response to each test item was also rated in terms of his fluency of language usage. By averaging the fluency ratings for these items it was possible to obtain an index for each child indicating his fluency in Spanish and English in responding to the test items.[1]

Prior to the broadcast of the 30-program series, each child was given two preseries tests, one in Spanish and one in English. The Spanish interview was conducted by a Mexican-American bilingual; the English testing was conducted by an Anglo-American monolingual speaker. Several weeks prior to testing, the interviewers spent regular amounts of time in the children's classrooms as teachers' assistants in order to become acquainted with the children and to increase potential rapport in the interview situation.

For testing, each child was taken from his classroom to an interview station, where informal remarks in the language of the interview were used as a warm-up. Subsequently the interviewer followed our predetermined format for eliciting the child's responses to the test items. Approximately half of the children had their English interview before the Spanish one, and vice versa, to avoid order effects. The two interviews conducted with each child were always separated by a period of several days. At the conclusion of each interview, the interviewer told the child that he had done well and gave him a small gift. Figure 3.1 shows the interview situation.

During periods when the program was broadcast, the children who had been selected for the viewer group went from their classrooms to a central viewing area, while children in the nonviewer group went to another area of the school. The viewing group received a selected warm-up of activities before the program, viewed the program, then usually engaged in follow-up activities before returning to the classroom.

Children in the nonviewer group were provided with an alternative activity in the form of a photography project. We thought it important that the children participate in an activity of high interest to them, lest they or their parents react negatively to their being excluded from the viewing group.

After the series of 30 programs, children participated in postseries interviews conducted in the same manner as the preseries pair. In scoring the tests, each child earned a point for each correct item and a fluency rating averaged from all items. For purposes of the present discussion these figures have been converted into percentage scores, although the statistical analyses were conducted on the frequency data. (The detailed frequency data, statistical models, and the like can be seen in the technical report of the project.)[2]

34

FIGURE 3.1

Interview Situation

Spanish Interview

English Interview

Results

Figures 3.2 and 3.3 summarize the percentage scores in the knowledge test areas of Spanish items for viewers and nonviewers in first and second grades. These percentage scores were slightly adjusted based on small differences found between the two groups in tests administered before the series. We examined the postseries scores to see where viewers and nonviewers differed to indicate effects of the program.

It was important in these interpretations to know how much of a difference in average scores between viewers and nonviewers constituted enough to be of interest to us. For this purpose, the results of statistical analyses can be applied that indicate the probability of whether any difference could occur simply from chance due to sampling. If the probability due to chance is relatively low (in this case, less than 5 percent), then the difference is "statistically significant" ($p < .05$), and we interpret it as an effect of the program. On the other hand, if the difference between viewers and nonviewers has greater than a 5 percent probability of occurring by chance, then we cannot be sure whether this is just a random fluctuation or is due to the effects of the program. In all of our interpretations in this study and others, we took the 5 percent level as a basis for estimating statistical significance. Viewer/nonviewer differences that are statistically significant are indicated by asterisks in all figures. Spanish-testing results indicated no statistically significant differences between the viewer/nonviewer groups in any comparison. Hence, it appeared that the program had no interpretable effects in the Spanish areas. Although we have not summarized the results here, all of the foregoing findings were similar for both traditional and bilingual classrooms.

Figures 3.4 and 3.5 summarize the same set of comparisons for results on the English testing. Results indicated that there were significant viewer/nonviewer differences in terms of the total knowledge score for second grade. In terms of the subtest scores of multicultural social environment (second grade), physical environment and concept development (first and second grades), gains were statistically significant.

Fluency percentage ratings of the children's responses to individual posttest items indicated a more positive rating of fluency for the viewer groups than for the nonviewers (Spanish viewers 84 percent, nonviewers 80 percent; English viewers 97 percent, nonviewers 92 percent). It appeared that viewing the program had an effect upon the child's fluency, as indexed in the test situation. However, it is important to interpret this result conservatively; presumably if a child knew the answers—and viewers in English tended to know more of the

FIGURE 3.2

PERCENTAGE GAINS IN SPANISH TEST ITEMS

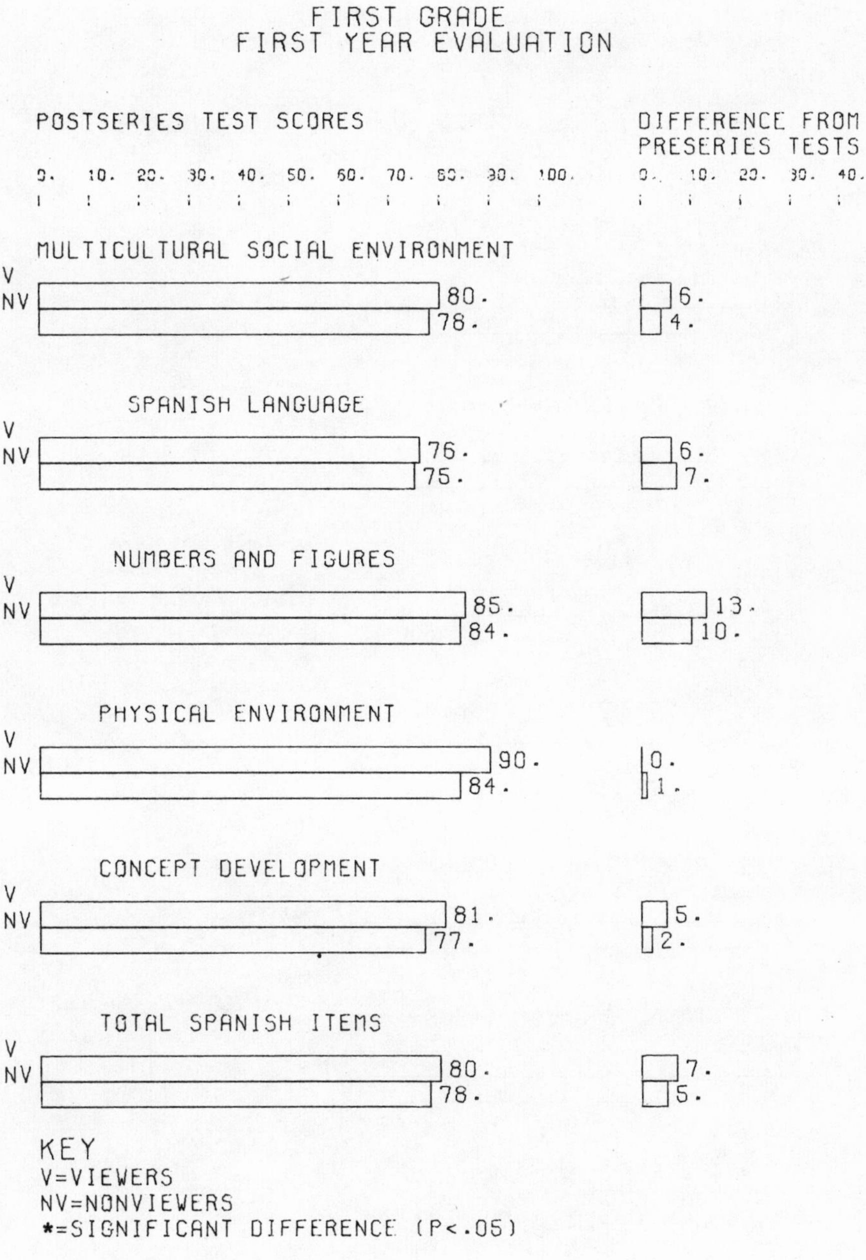

FIRST GRADE
FIRST YEAR EVALUATION

POSTSERIES TEST SCORES

DIFFERENCE FROM
PRESERIES TESTS

0. 10. 20. 30. 40. 50. 60. 70. 80. 90. 100.   0. 10. 20. 30. 40.

MULTICULTURAL SOCIAL ENVIRONMENT

V
NV   80.   6.
       78.   4.

SPANISH LANGUAGE

V
NV   76.   6.
       75.   7.

NUMBERS AND FIGURES

V
NV   85.   13.
       84.   10.

PHYSICAL ENVIRONMENT

V
NV   90.   0.
       84.   1.

CONCEPT DEVELOPMENT

V
NV   81.   5.
       77.   2.

TOTAL SPANISH ITEMS

V
NV   80.   7.
       78.   5.

KEY
V=VIEWERS
NV=NONVIEWERS
*=SIGNIFICANT DIFFERENCE (P<.05)

37

FIGURE 3.3

PERCENTAGE GAINS IN SPANISH TEST ITEMS

SECOND GRADE
FIRST YEAR EVALUATION

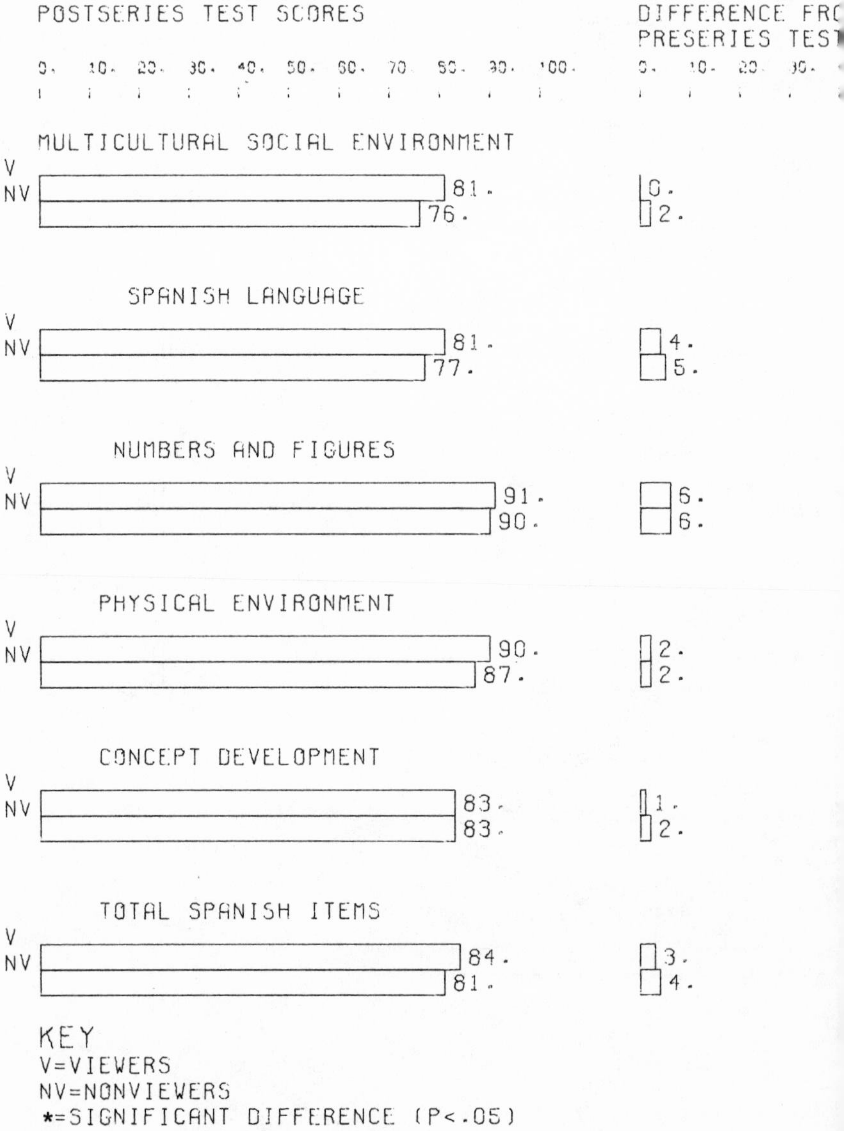

POSTSERIES TEST SCORES

DIFFERENCE FR
PRESERIES TES1

0.   10. 20. 30. 40. 50. 60. 70. 80. 90. 100.

0.   10. 20. 30.

MULTICULTURAL SOCIAL ENVIRONMENT

V
NV
81.
76.

0.
2.

SPANISH LANGUAGE

V
NV
81.
77.

4.
5.

NUMBERS AND FIGURES

V
NV
91.
90.

6.
6.

PHYSICAL ENVIRONMENT

V
NV
90.
87.

2.
2.

CONCEPT DEVELOPMENT

V
NV
83.
83.

1.
2.

TOTAL SPANISH ITEMS

V
NV
84.
81.

3.
4.

KEY
V=VIEWERS
NV=NONVIEWERS
*=SIGNIFICANT DIFFERENCE (P<.05)

FIGURE 3.4

PERCENTAGE GAINS IN ENGLISH TEST ITEMS

FIRST GRADE
FIRST YEAR EVALUATION

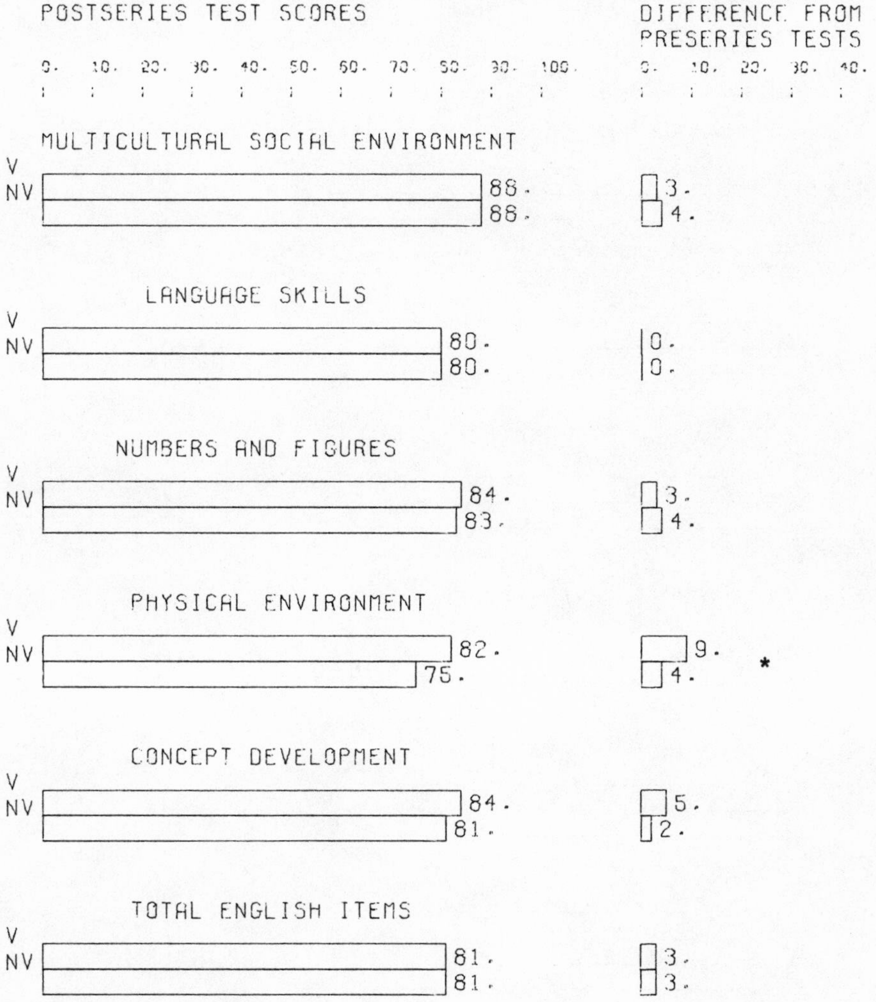

POSTSERIES TEST SCORES

0. 10. 20. 30. 40. 50. 60. 70. 80. 90. 100.

DIFFERENCE FROM
PRESERIES TESTS

0. 10. 20. 30. 40.

MULTICULTURAL SOCIAL ENVIRONMENT
V
NV
88.
88.
3.
4.

LANGUAGE SKILLS
V
NV
80.
80.
0.
0.

NUMBERS AND FIGURES
V
NV
84.
83.
3.
4.

PHYSICAL ENVIRONMENT
V
NV
82.
75.
9.   *
4.

CONCEPT DEVELOPMENT
V
NV
84.
81.
5.
2.

TOTAL ENGLISH ITEMS
V
NV
81.
81.
3.
3.

KEY
V=VIEWERS
NV=NONVIEWERS
*=SIGNIFICANT DIFFERENCE (P<.05)

FIGURE 3.5

PERCENTAGE GAINS IN ENGLISH TEST ITEMS

SECOND GRADE
FIRST YEAR EVALUATION

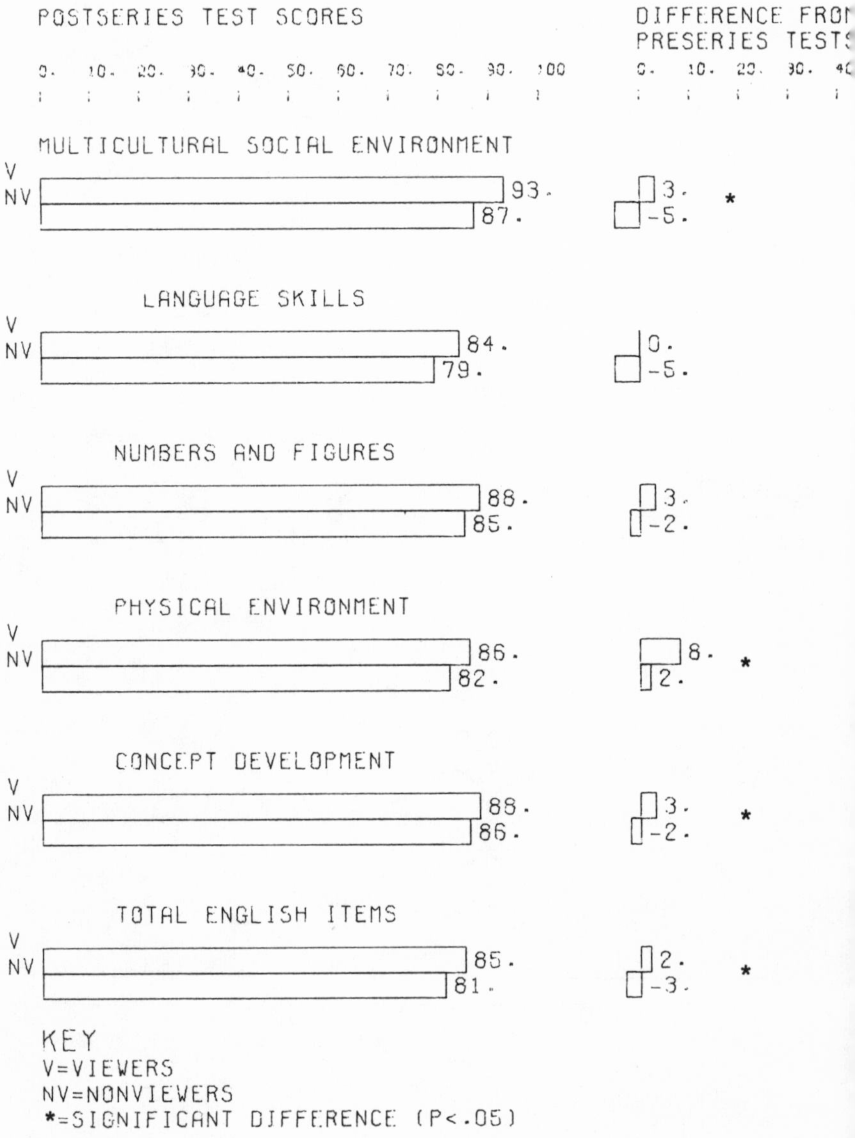

POSTSERIES TEST SCORES

DIFFERENCE FROM
PRESERIES TESTS

0. 10. 20. 30. 40. 50. 60. 70. 80. 90. 100

0. 10. 20. 30. 40

MULTICULTURAL SOCIAL ENVIRONMENT

V
NV

93.

87.

3. *

-5.

LANGUAGE SKILLS

V
NV

84.

79.

0.

-5.

NUMBERS AND FIGURES

V
NV

88.

85.

3.

-2.

PHYSICAL ENVIRONMENT

V
NV

86.

82.

8. *

2.

CONCEPT DEVELOPMENT

V
NV

88.

86.

3. *

-2.

TOTAL ENGLISH ITEMS

V
NV

85.

81.

2. *

-3.

KEY
V=VIEWERS
NV=NONVIEWERS
*=SIGNIFICANT DIFFERENCE (P<.05)

answers—he would be more fluent in giving them. Thus fluency ratings may not reflect a lack of hesitance in speech, but may also indirectly reflect some of the positive knowledge gains of the viewer groups.

THE SECOND YEAR

Research Design

The second year's experiment was again conducted at Zavala Elementary School, but this time it was restricted to first graders in bilingual classrooms, who as kindergartners the year before had not regularly viewed the program. These children were randomly assigned to one of three research groups: (1) viewers who had supplementary classroom activities relevant to the program, (2) viewers who had no classroom activities directly relevant to the program, and (3) a group of children who were nonviewers. The experiment was completed by 44 pupils divided into the three groups.

Again test items were developed by sampling from the Spanish and English behavioral objectives of the television series.[3]

The test items were sampled from seven content areas: Spanish language skills, phoneme/grapheme relationships, math (treated exclusively in Spanish); science, history/culture, self-concept (treated in either Spanish or English); and English language skills. Although math items were taught only in Spanish, they were included in both Spanish and English tests to see the degree to which there would be carry-over from the Spanish language instruction. Where the behavioral objectives were the same in the first-year series, some test items were carried over from the first year's testing.

As in the first year, tests were administered individually to each child by one bilingual Mexican-American (Spanish test) and one Anglo-American (English test). Separate test interviews in the two languages were conducted before the program series and after ten weeks following the series. A fluency measure was again calculated, based on evaluation of the child's response to the questions requiring continuous answers. The nonviewer group was engaged in a photography class during the period that the "Carrascolendas" programs were on the air as in the first year.

Results

Figure 3.6 summarizes the percentage test scores in Spanish across all items and for each subcategory. Within the comparison

FIGURE 3.6

PERCENTAGE GAINS IN SPANISH TEST ITEMS
SECOND YEAR EVALUATION

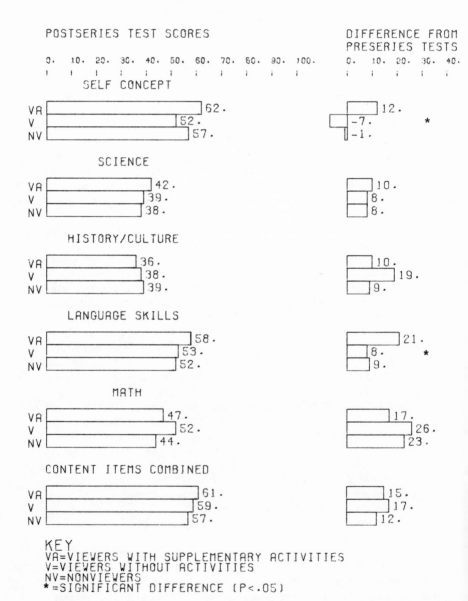

POSTSERIES TEST SCORES

DIFFERENCE FROM
PRESERIES TESTS

0. 10. 20. 30. 40. 50. 60. 70. 80. 90. 100. 0. 10. 20. 30. 40.

SELF CONCEPT

VA 62.   12.
V 52.   -7.   *
NV 57.   -1.

SCIENCE

VA 42.   10.
V 39.   8.
NV 38.   8.

HISTORY/CULTURE

VA 36.   10.
V 38.   19.
NV 39.   9.

LANGUAGE SKILLS

VA 58.   21.
V 53.   8.   *
NV 52.   9.

MATH

VA 47.   17.
V 52.   26.
NV 44.   23.

CONTENT ITEMS COMBINED

VA 61.   15.
V 59.   17.
NV 57.   12.

KEY
VA=VIEWERS WITH SUPPLEMENTARY ACTIVITIES
V=VIEWERS WITHOUT ACTIVITIES
NV=NONVIEWERS
*=SIGNIFICANT DIFFERENCE (P<.05)

42

of the three groups, the differences indicated that although the two viewer groups slightly exceeded the nonviewer groups in combined scores, the difference among these averages was no better than a chance occurrence. An examination of the subtest scores indicates statistically significant differences in measures of self-concept and language skills. For both self-concept and language skills, the viewer groups with activities significantly exceeded both the group without activities and the nonviewer group.

Figure 3.7 summarizes the postseries test scores in the English area. Here results indicated that viewers with supplementary activities usually made better overall scores than viewers who had no activities. In all but the self-concept category, the viewers (no activities) in turn exceeded the nonviewers. Statistical analyses of differences among the three groups in the subtest scores indicated significant differences in the history/culture and language-skill areas. Although the probability of the averages differing by chance was slightly greater than the criterion level set for significance, differences in science and math were greater for viewers with activities and, in the case of science, for viewing alone. But in all, the overall differences in the English test items were mainly due to items in the history/culture and language-skills areas. There were no differences favoring the viewer group in the measures of self-concept; indeed, the nonviewer's scores tended to exceed the other two groups.

As discussed earlier, whenever a child was given a test item that could be expected to prompt more than a single word responses, a fluency rating was assigned on a one to four scale. Figure 3.8 summarizes the average ratings of different test groups. Results of the statistical analyses indicated that the greatest ratings of fluency for both the English and Spanish test items were from the viewer groups that had activities. Some of these differences, however, were not significant, but pointed to a somewhat greater fluency for the viewers, particularly those with activities.

THE THIRD YEAR

Research Design

The third year's evaluation of "Carrascolendas" took place at test sites located in concentrations of Mexican-American populations in different parts of the United States. Texas was again included, but test sites were located in a major urban area (San Antonio) as well as in a small city (Edinburg) that is representative of Mexican-Americans living in the Rio Grande Valley. In this chapter we will report

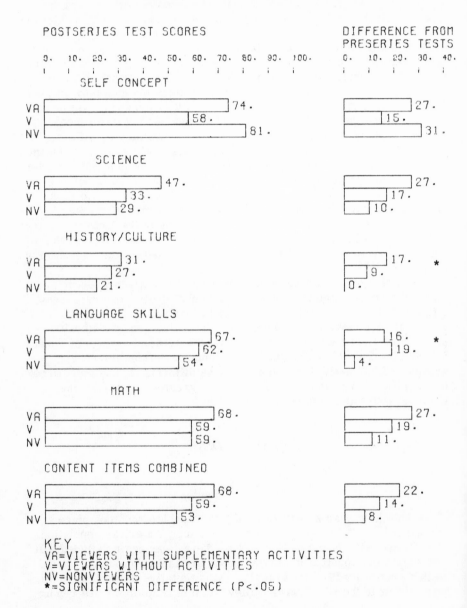

FIGURE 3.7

PERCENTAGE GAINS IN ENGLISH TEST ITEMS

SECOND YEAR EVALUATION

POSTSERIES TEST SCORES

DIFFERENCE FROM
PRESERIES TESTS

KEY
VR=VIEWERS WITH SUPPLEMENTARY ACTIVITIES
V=VIEWERS WITHOUT ACTIVITIES
NV=NONVIEWERS
*=SIGNIFICANT DIFFERENCE (P<.05)

44

FIGURE 3.8

FLUENCY AVERAGES
ON A 1-4 SCALE

SECOND YEAR EVALUATION

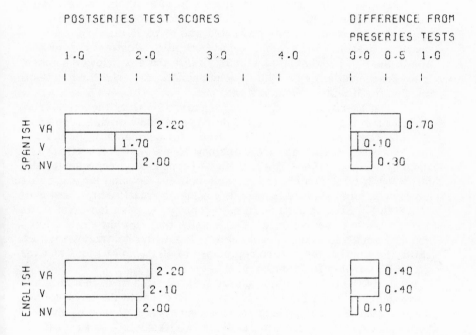

POSTSERIES TEST SCORES

DIFFERENCE FROM
PRESERIES TESTS

KEY
VA=VIEWERS WITH SUPPLEMENTARY ACTIVITIES
V=VIEWERS WITHOUT ACTIVITIES
NV=NONVIEWERS
*=SIGNIFICANT DIFFERENCE (P<.05)

on the Texas sites; the remaining sites are discussed in the next chapter.

The kindergarten, first, and second-grade children at the San Antonio site consisted of two viewer groups from different elementary schools and one nonviewer group. Both schools participate in a Title VII bilingual program. The ethnicity of the San Antonio schools involved in the evaluation was a combined total of 98 percent Mexican-American children. In rural Edinburg, viewer and nonviewer subjects in kindergarten and second grade came from one elementary school and first-grade viewers and nonviewers from another. Both schools had predominantly Mexican-American student populations. The original number of students pretested was to be 15 viewers and 5 nonviewers from each grade level at each site. Posttest measurements were to be completed with 12 viewer and 4 nonviewer subjects from every grade level. The smaller number assigned for posttesting allowed for illness or school transfers.

Test items for the third year's evaluation were the same at all test sites in the United States. This represented a revised version of the second year's test, omitting items for segments of the series that had been dropped and including new items for occasional insertions of new segments. The test items (Appendix A) represented the following Spanish content areas: self-concept, Spanish language skills, history/culture, science, phoneme/grapheme relationships, and math. Those in the English area were self-concept, English language skills, history/culture, and science. The Spanish tests for the third year had 52 items, requiring approximately 30 minutes to administer to a child; the English tests were comprised of 40 items and took an average of 25 minutes to administer.

As in the prior studies, children at all sites were tested individually in Spanish and English; testers were fluent in the language of the test administered. Three or more days were allowed to elapse between tests. Pretesting began about two weeks before Program 1 was aired and posttesting usually followed viewing of Program 30. However, due to air date variations, some posttesting was begun after Program 27. Test instruments, designed with this possibility in mind, did not include items treated exclusively in the last three programs of the series.

Field consultants were engaged to contact schools and local television stations. They also hired and trained the field agents who conducted the interviews for data collections. The agents were trained in interview techniques with children for gathering field experiment data and with parents for the telephone survey eliciting attitude data. It was recommended that all agents spend time in the classrooms before testing and conduct two or three sample interviews with children who were not experimental subjects. Tests were to be administered in relatively private areas of the school, so that the children's attention would not be diverted from the test items. However, some sites had difficulty in securing good locations. Efforts were made throughout the interview situation to maintain a relaxed atmosphere; additional remarks addressed to the children were made in the same language of the test being conducted.

In the second year's research, a scoring procedure was developed that differentiated not only right from wrong responses, but added a weighting for degree of correctness. (A perfect response was weighted as "4," a prompted response "3," a partially correct response "2," and an incorrect or no response "1.")

Results

Figures 3.9 and 3.10 summarize the results of the children's responses to the Spanish and English tests at the San Antonio sites. These results are displayed in terms of individual content areas of the test and as a total representing a combination of content areas. With the exception of the phoneme/grapheme measures shown in Figure 3.9, the viewer group consistently exceeded nonviewers in score gains from tests administered before viewing the entire series compared to tests administered after completion of the series. Results of the statistical analyses indicated that on the total Spanish scores, the viewer/nonviewer differences were not statistically significant, but for the English items there was a significant difference in total score between the viewer and nonviewer groups. In the Spanish test items the subjects in the area of history/culture and science significantly favored the viewer group, and math was close to being statistically significant. On the other hand, the difference in gains between the viewer and nonviewer groups in phoneme/grapheme relationships was statistically significant, but favored the nonviewer group. In terms of subtests for English items, the science subtest was statistically significant in the comparisons of the viewer/nonviewer groups. The comparison in the history/culture items came close to the level of significance.

Edinburg children's average degrees of correctness on the test items are summarized in Figures 3.11 and 3.12, representing the Spanish and English tests respectively. Again, the average scores consistently favored the viewer groups over the nonviewers, although not all such differences were greater than chance. The most substantial result was that the total test scores in both the Spanish and English tests for Edinburg children were statistically significant and favored the viewer group over the nonviewer. In the Spanish subtests the history/culture items showed a significant difference

47

FIGURE 3.9

AVERAGE DEGREE OF CORRECTNESS IN SPANISH TEST ITEMS SAN ANTONIO

THIRD YEAR EVALUATION

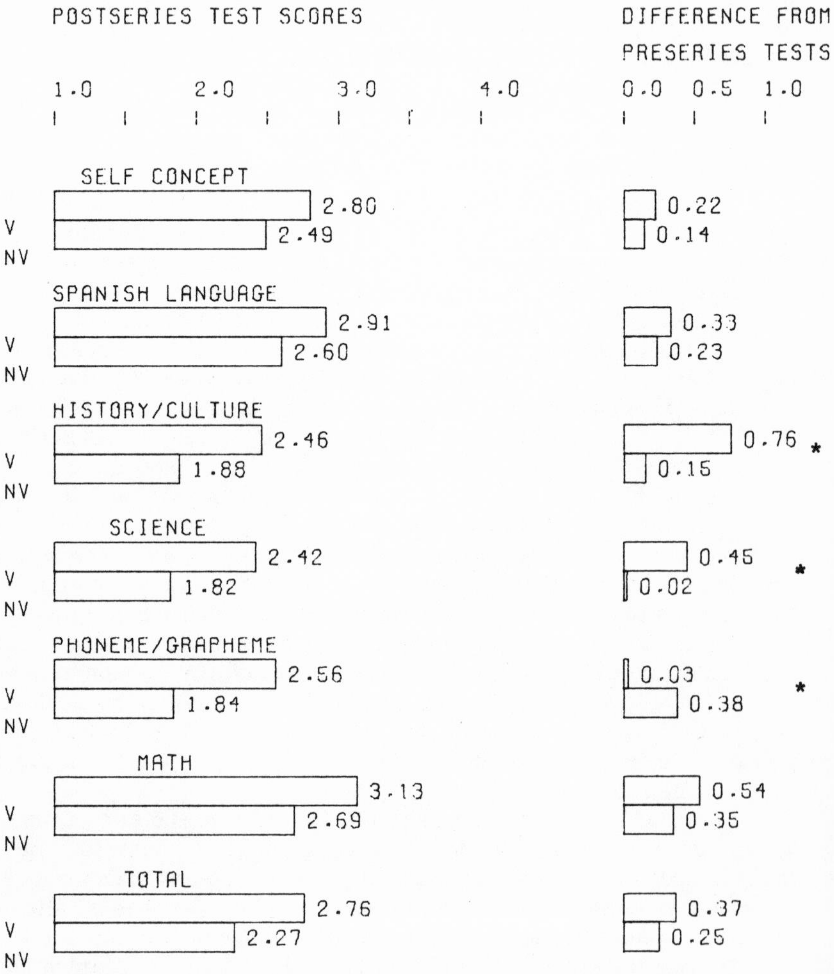

POSTSERIES TEST SCORES

DIFFERENCE FROM PRESERIES TESTS

1.0	2.0	3.0	4.0	0.0 0.5 1.0

SELF CONCEPT

V 2.80   0.22
NV 2.49   0.14

SPANISH LANGUAGE

V 2.91   0.33
NV 2.60   0.23

HISTORY/CULTURE

V 2.46   0.76 *
NV 1.88   0.15

SCIENCE

V 2.42   0.45 *
NV 1.82   0.02

PHONEME/GRAPHEME

V 2.56   0.03 *
NV 1.84   0.38

MATH

V 3.13   0.54
NV 2.69   0.35

TOTAL

V 2.76   0.37
NV 2.27   0.25

KEY

V=VIEWERS

NV=NONVIEWERS

*=SIGNIFICANT DIFFERENCE (P<.05)

FIGURE 3.10

AVERAGE DEGREE OF CORRECTNESS
IN ENGLISH TEST ITEMS
SAN ANTONIO

THIRD YEAR EVALUATION

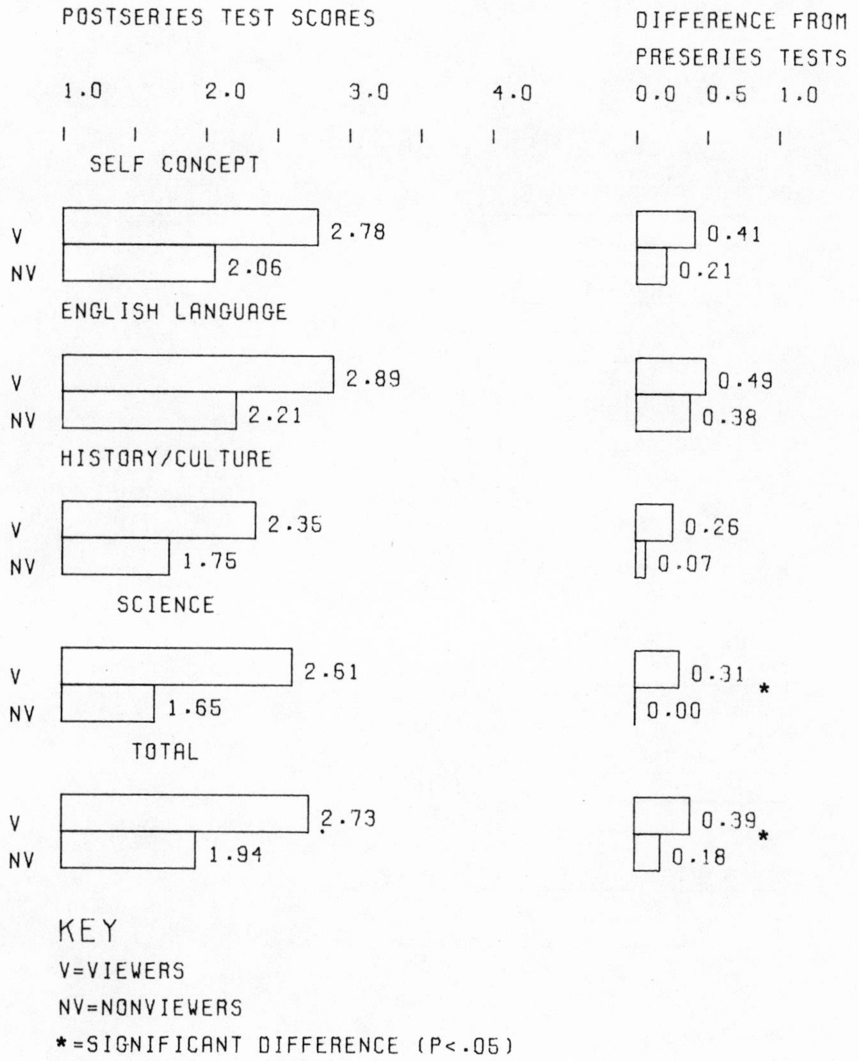

POSTSERIES TEST SCORES

DIFFERENCE FROM
PRESERIES TESTS

| 1.0 | 2.0 | 3.0 | 4.0 | 0.0 | 0.5 | 1.0 |

SELF CONCEPT

V — 2.78 — 0.41
NV — 2.06 — 0.21

ENGLISH LANGUAGE

V — 2.89 — 0.49
NV — 2.21 — 0.38

HISTORY/CULTURE

V — 2.35 — 0.26
NV — 1.75 — 0.07

SCIENCE

V — 2.61 — 0.31 *
NV — 1.65 — 0.00

TOTAL

V — 2.73 — 0.39 *
NV — 1.94 — 0.18

KEY
V=VIEWERS
NV=NONVIEWERS
*=SIGNIFICANT DIFFERENCE (P<.05)

FIGURE 3.11
AVERAGE DEGREE OF CORRECTNESS
IN SPANISH TEST ITEMS
EDINBURG

THIRD YEAR EVALUATION

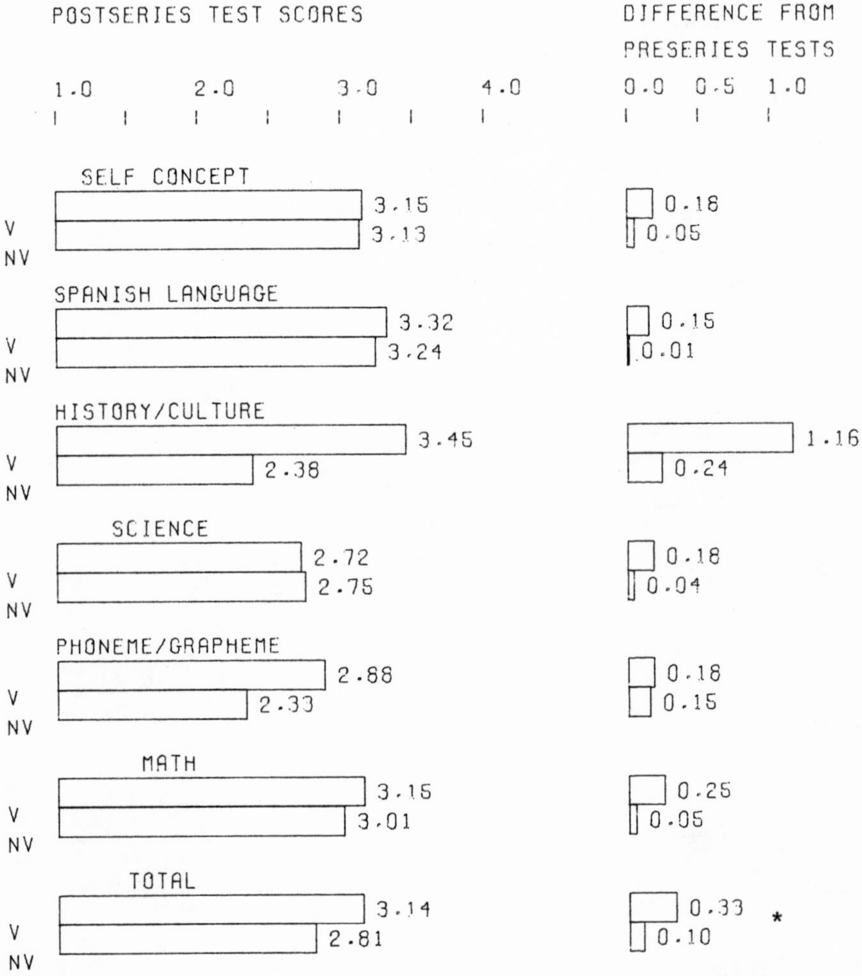

POSTSERIES TEST SCORES

DIFFERENCE FROM
PRESERIES TESTS

| 1.0 | 2.0 | 3.0 | 4.0 | 0.0 0.5 1.0 |

SELF CONCEPT

V 3.15 — 0.18
NV 3.13 — 0.05

SPANISH LANGUAGE

V 3.32 — 0.15
NV 3.24 — 0.01

HISTORY/CULTURE

V 3.45 — 1.16
NV 2.38 — 0.24

SCIENCE

V 2.72 — 0.18
NV 2.75 — 0.04

PHONEME/GRAPHEME

V 2.88 — 0.18
NV 2.33 — 0.15

MATH

V 3.15 — 0.25
NV 3.01 — 0.05

TOTAL

V 3.14 — 0.33 *
NV 2.81 — 0.10

KEY
V=VIEWERS
NV=NONVIEWERS
*=SIGNIFICANT DIFFERENCE (P<.05)

FIGURE 3.12

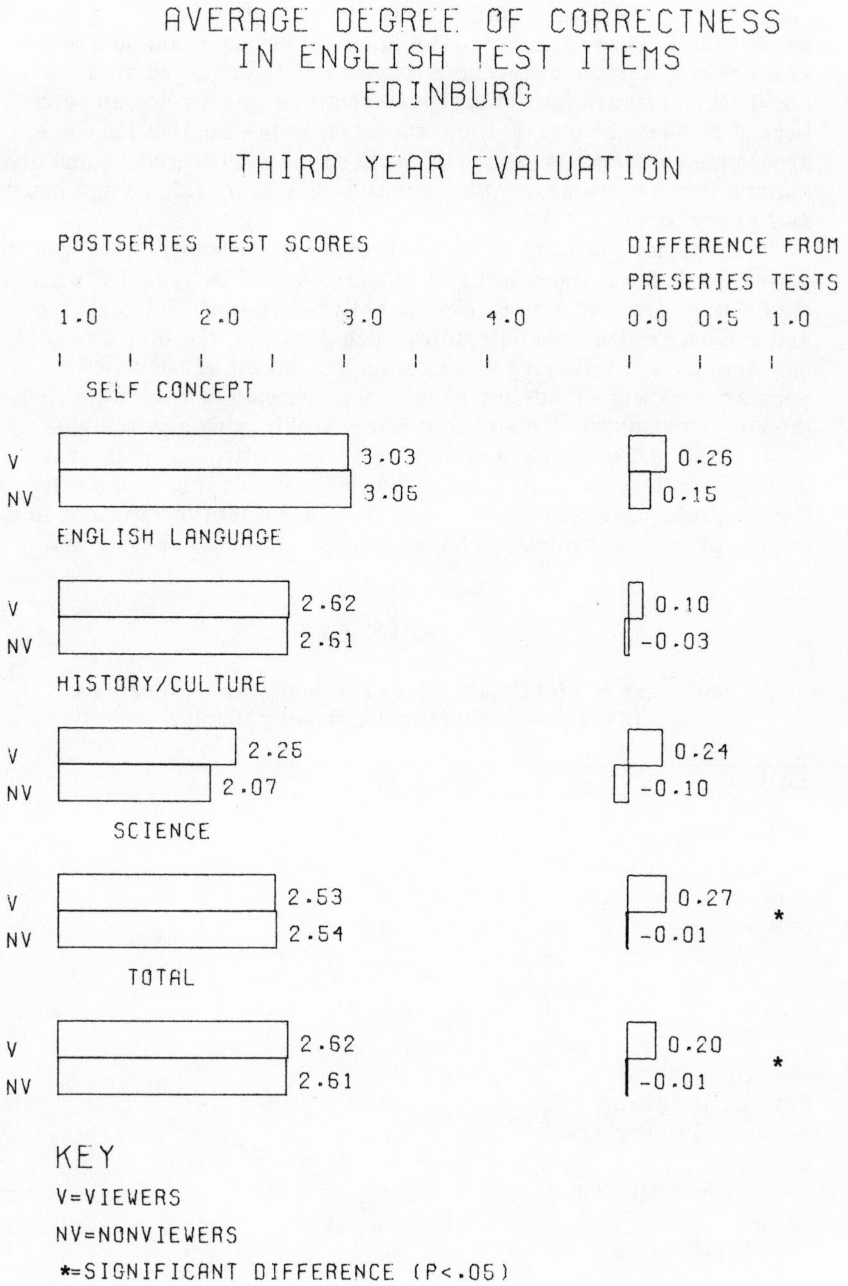

AVERAGE DEGREE OF CORRECTNESS
IN ENGLISH TEST ITEMS
EDINBURG

THIRD YEAR EVALUATION

| POSTSERIES TEST SCORES | | | | DIFFERENCE FROM PRESERIES TESTS | | |

SELF CONCEPT

V — 3.03   0.26
NV — 3.05   0.15

ENGLISH LANGUAGE

V — 2.62   0.10
NV — 2.61   -0.03

HISTORY/CULTURE

V — 2.25   0.24
NV — 2.07   -0.10

SCIENCE

V — 2.53   0.27 *
NV — 2.54   -0.01

TOTAL

V — 2.62   0.20 *
NV — 2.61   -0.01

KEY
V=VIEWERS
NV=NONVIEWERS
*=SIGNIFICANT DIFFERENCE (P<.05)

between viewers and nonviewers. Also the difference in Spanish language skills was nearly statistically significant (p = < .12 against the needed .05). Thus, similar to the Spanish test data obtained in previous years, certain differences were revealed between viewers and nonviewers and all such differences could be interpreted as being beyond chance. In terms of the subtests, in the English language area, science items statistically favored the viewer groups and history/ culture items were nearly statistically significant (.08 as against the necessary .05).

A further question in the analysis of the Texas results was whether patterns of viewer/nonviewer differences would be revealed when the data were examined separately for children in kindergarten, first, and second grades. To determine such patterns, the test data from San Antonio and Edinburg were combined and viewer/nonviewer comparisons were made for each of the subtests and the total tests; the comparisons were made separately within each grade level.

Table 3.1 presents a summary of the findings in each of the three grade levels. Inspection of the table shows that in the third-year Texas sites, "Carrascolendas" had the least effect on children in the second grade and seemed to have about the same number of, but

TABLE 3.1

Summary of Significant Viewer/Nonviewer Differences
(X) in San Antonio and Edinburg Results

English	K	1	2
Self-Concept	—	—	—
English Language	X	—	—
History/Culture	—	X	—
Science	X	X	—
Total	X	X	—
Spanish			
Self-Concept	—	X	—
Spanish Language	—	—	—
History/Culture	X	—	X
Science	—	—	—
Phoneme/Grapheme	—	—	—
Math	—	—	—
Total	X	—	—

FIGURE 3.13

FLUENCY AVERAGES
ON A 1-4 SCALE

THIRD YEAR EVALUATION

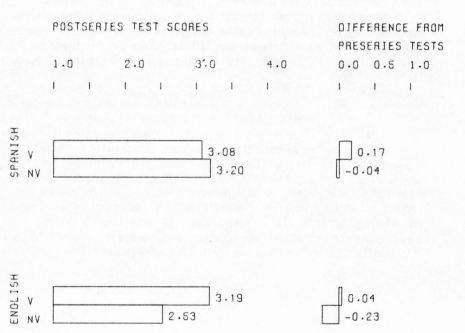

POSTSERIES TEST SCORES

DIFFERENCE FROM
PRESERIES TESTS

| 1.0 | 2.0 | 3.0 | 4.0 | 0.0 | 0.5 | 1.0 |

SPANISH

V 3.08   0.17
NV 3.20   -0.04

ENGLISH

V 3.19   0.04
NV 2.53   -0.23

KEY
V=VIEWERS WITHOUT ACTIVITIES
NV=NONVIEWERS
*=SIGNIFICANT DIFFERENCE (P<.05)

different, effects on children in kindergarten and first grade. Again, as found in previous analyses, differences favoring the viewer groups were found more often in the English area than in the Spanish area. The differences in the English area were statistically significant in total scores for both kindergarten and first graders. These results could be practically applied in disseminating the series when we are concerned with the types of children who might view it in the state of Texas. Evaluation evidence indicates a more consistent impact with kindergartners and first graders than with second graders.

Figure 3.13 summarizes the fluency ratings of the San Antonio and Edinburg test groups. In comparing differences between viewers and nonviewers, no statistically significant gains were evident in terms of fluency. However, viewers again indicated greater fluency than nonviewers.

SOME GENERALIZATIONS

Results in Texas over the three years indicated significant gains made by viewers in different content areas when compared to nonviewers. Gains in the first year of testing were significant in first and second grades in English areas only. However, during the second and third years, gains were evident in both English and Spanish, although in different content areas. When children's fluency measures were compared, viewers generally achieved greater fluency than nonviewers, although gains were not statistically significant.

NOTES

1. Copies of the tests for the first year may be found in Diana S. Natalicio and Frederick Williams, Carracolendas: Evaluation of a Bilingual Television Series, Grant No. OEG-09-530094-4239-(280), U.S. Department of Health, Education, and Welfare, Office of Education (Austin, Texas: Center for Communication Research, 1971).

2. Ibid.

3. Copies of the tests for the second year may be found in Frederick Williams, Susan McRae, and Geraldine Van Wart, Carrascolendas: Effects of a Spanish/English Television Series for Primary School Children, Grant No. OEG-09-530094-4239-(280), U.S. Department of Health, Education, and Welfare, Office of Education (Austin, Texas: Center for Communication Research, 1972).

4

**EFFECTS ON
THE CHILDREN:
THE NATIONAL STUDY**

GOALS

The evaluation in the third year involved conducting field experiments in schools in addition to the sites chosen in Texas that were described in Chapter 3. These included two sites in California: one rural (Tracy) and one urban (Los Angeles). Lansing, Michigan was chosen as a site in order to sample children of migrant Mexican-American families. The sites in the Southwest were located at Albuquerque, New Mexico; Tucson, Arizona; Pueblo, Colorado;* Edinburg (rural and San Antonio (urban), Texas.

Because the contractual arrangements for the third-year evaluation were not completed until late July 1972, only a short time was available for planning. This involved selecting at each site a field consultant and a staff for testing, obtaining school permission for such testing, and arranging for a public broadcasting station to air the program regularly during school hours in the fall season. Field consultant training took place in August, pretesting of the children took place in September, the series began in October, and posttesting was conducted in December, at the end of 27 programs of the 30-program series.

TEST SITES

Sixteen schools in eight states participated in the testing. Their characteristics are summarized in Appendix B. All of the schools

---

*Originally, Denver had been selected as a site; however, due to the failure of the field agent to carry out instructions in that area, the site was shifted to Pueblo.

except Lansing, Pueblo, Tracy, and one of the three in Albuquerque
had ongoing, bilingual programs. Thus, the viewing of "Carrascolendas"
in such schools was part of a variety of bilingual educational materials
and strategies. At most of these schools, teachers were fluent in
Spanish. In contrast, schools lacking a bilingual program contained
groups of Mexican-American children for whom "Carrascolendas"
was presumably the only exposure to bilingual educational materials.
The Pueblo site had two special study components of interest to us—a
group of third-grade Mexican-American children and a group of Anglo
children. Finally it should be noted that only in San Antonio and Tucson
was the series viewed in color; all other schools viewed in black and
white.

At each site the field experiment was to include 15 viewers in
each of kindergarten, first, and second grades and 5 nonviewers in
each of these grades. It was assumed that if posttest measurements
could be completed with a minimum of 12 viewers and 4 nonviewers
for each grade level, this would be sufficient for the data analysis.
For the most part this was accomplished, and eventually there were
totals of 340 viewer children and 106 nonviewer children whose tests
gains were available for comparison.

As described in more detail in Chapter 3, measurement instruments were developed from a sampling of the behavioral objectives
of "Carrascolendas." The test (see Appendix A) included 44 behavioral
objectives that were tested in Spanish and 30 tested in English. The
behavioral objectives were divided among the subtest areas of history/
culture, self-concept, science, and English for the English test sequence
and the first three of those areas plus math, phoneme/grapheme
relationships, and Spanish for the Spanish test sequence. The weighted
scoring scheme was again used where a perfect response was a "4,"
a prompted response "3," a partial response "2," and an incorrect
or no response "1."

Testing was accomplished in the national study in much the
same way as in the first two years, as was described in Chapter 3.
The main difference in the national study was that most of the training
of test personnel was done by field consultants who, in turn, were
instructed by the central project staff. Although this could lead to
greater error in test administration visits to sites and double checking
of test scoring indicated that the results were sufficiently accurate
for interpretation.

RESULTS

Overall Scores

Figure 4.1 presents the total Spanish and English test results for each site; for purposes of comparison we will include the results of the Texas sites discussed in the last chapter. In all, effects of the program across different sites were about equally divided between the Spanish and English test areas. The general results may be summarized as follows:

1. The only significant gains found in the Spanish testings were for the viewers in the monolingual Albuquerque classrooms, in Edinburg, and the Mexican-American Pueblo classrooms.

2. Similar significant gains in the English area were found in Edinburg, Los Angeles, the monolingual San Antonio classrooms, and Tracy.

3. No evidence of significant gains were found between viewers and nonviewers in the bilingual Albuquerque and San Antonio classrooms, in Lansing, the Anglo Pueblo classrooms, and Tucson.

As anticipated, these results indicate that if significant differences in gains are to be found between viewers and nonviewers, they will typically favor the viewer group. On the other hand, such differences varied substantially across the different sites in comparison of the Spanish and English areas. In interpreting these results, it should be noted that overall score comparisons were first used with no distinction according to grade levels or subject content. At best, then, the results shown in Figure 4.1 only gauge the overall impact of the program in Spanish and English areas at the different test sites.

Differences by Grades

Figure 4.2 summarizes the posttest average scores in the Spanish area for viewers and nonviewers in each of the three grade levels tested nationally and for all three grades combined. These combinations include the Texas data. As in the previous section the focus is upon viewer/nonviewer comparisons. Posttest scores are given, but the main statistical comparison is between viewers and nonviewers in terms of gains that these posttest scores represent over pretest scores. Again, the scoring uses the 1-4 scale given earlier. In Figure 4.2 we see that in the analysis of the data, viewer test averages significantly exceeded nonviewer averages at a level beyond chance only for first graders and in the combined grades.

FIGURE 4.1

COMPARISONS OF VIEWER AND NONVIEWER COMBINED SCORE GAINS AT EIGHT TEST SITES

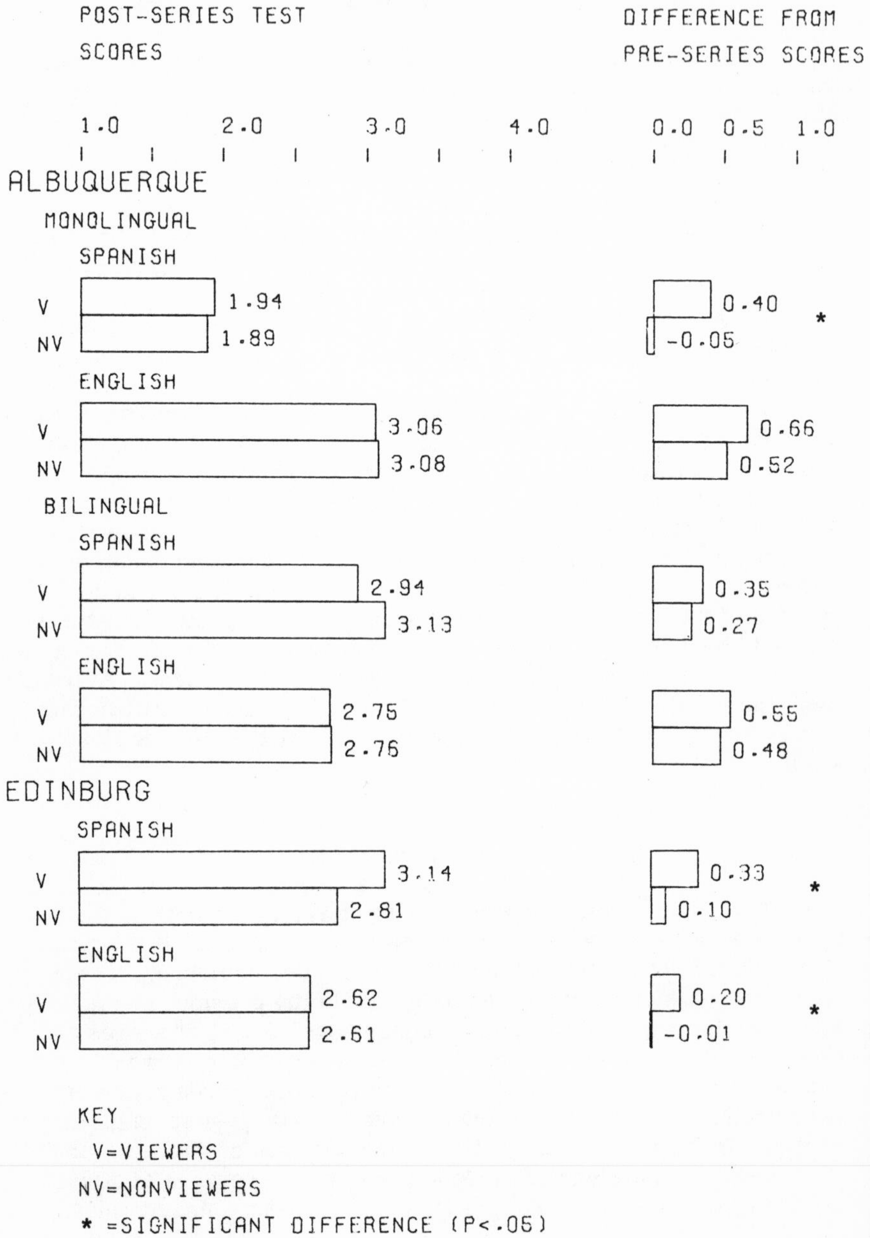
POST-SERIES TEST SCORES
DIFFERENCE FROM PRE-SERIES SCORES
1.0
2.0
3.0
4.0
0.0
0.5
1.0
ALBUQUERQUE
MONOLINGUAL
SPANISH
V
1.94
0.40
*
NV
1.89
-0.05
ENGLISH
V
3.06
0.66
NV
3.08
0.52
BILINGUAL
SPANISH
V
2.94
0.35
NV
3.13
0.27
ENGLISH
V
2.75
0.55
NV
2.76
0.48
EDINBURG
SPANISH
V
3.14
0.33
*
NV
2.81
0.10
ENGLISH
V
2.62
0.20
*
NV
2.61
-0.01
KEY
V=VIEWERS
NV=NONVIEWERS
* =SIGNIFICANT DIFFERENCE (P<.05)

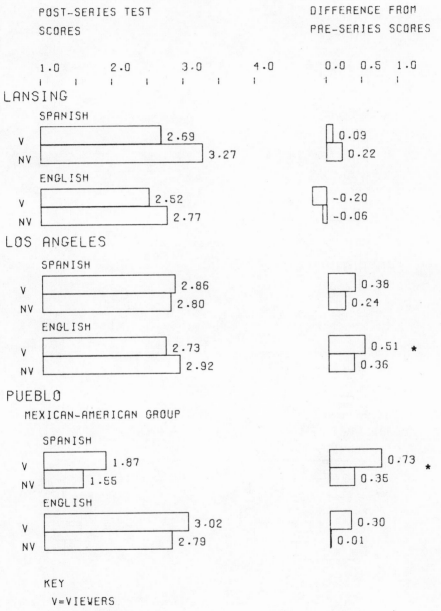

FIGURE 4.1 (Continued)

COMPARISONS OF VIEWER AND NONVIEWER
COMBINED SCORE GAINS AT EIGHT TEST SITES

POST-SERIES TEST   DIFFERENCE FROM
SCORES   PRE-SERIES SCORES

1.0   2.0   3.0   4.0   0.0 0.5 1.0

LANSING

SPANISH

V   2.69   0.09
NV   3.27   0.22

ENGLISH

V   2.52   -0.20
NV   2.77   -0.06

LOS ANGELES

SPANISH

V   2.86   0.38
NV   2.80   0.24

ENGLISH

V   2.73   0.51 *
NV   2.92   0.36

PUEBLO

MEXICAN-AMERICAN GROUP

SPANISH

V   1.87   0.73 *
NV   1.55   0.35

ENGLISH

V   3.02   0.30
NV   2.79   0.01

KEY

V=VIEWERS

NV=NONVIEWERS

* =SIGNIFICANT DIFFERENCE (P<.05)

59

FIGURE 4.1 (Continued)

COMPARISONS OF VIEWER AND NONVIEWER
COMBINED SCORE GAINS AT EIGHT TEST SITES

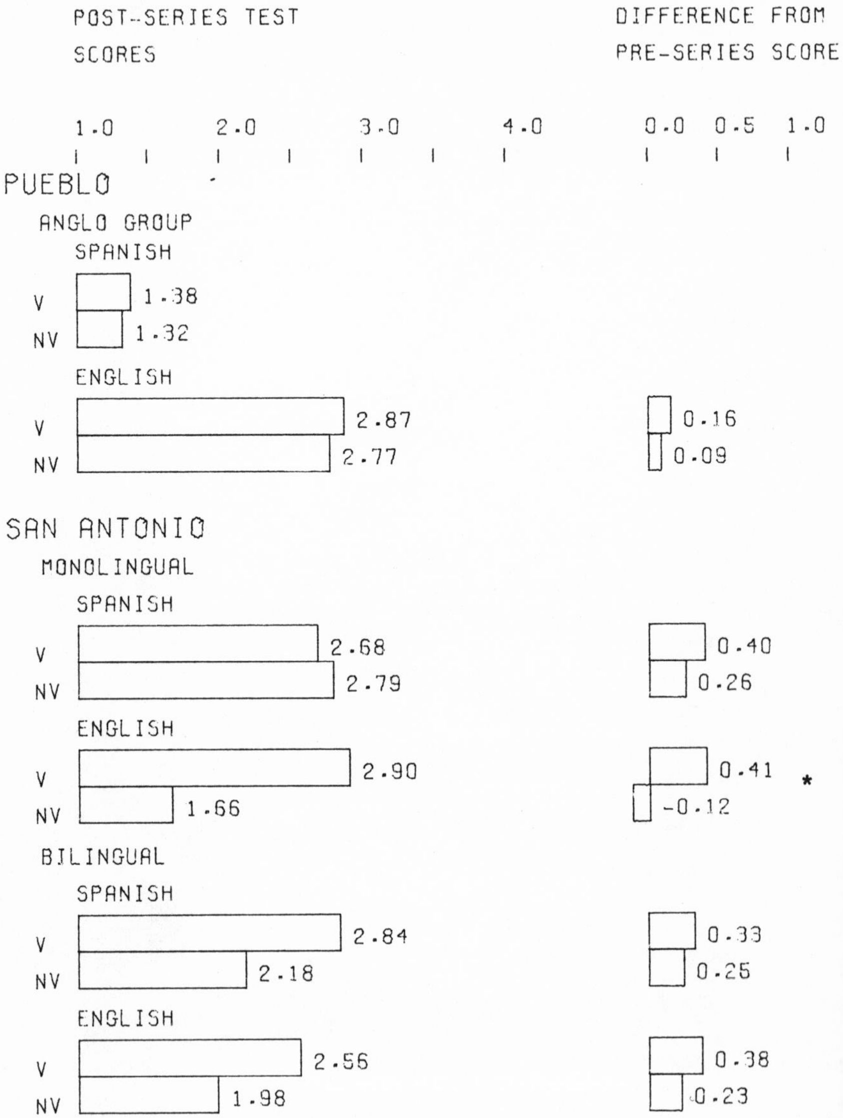

POST-SERIES TEST   DIFFERENCE FROM
SCORES   PRE-SERIES SCORE

```
        1.0      2.0      3.0      4.0      0.0  0.5  1.0
        |    |    |    |    |    |    |      |    |    |
PUEBLO          ·
  ANGLO GROUP
     SPANISH
  V  [    ] 1.38
  NV [   ] 1.32

     ENGLISH
  V  [              ] 2.87          [ ] 0.16
  NV [             ] 2.77           [ ] 0.09

SAN ANTONIO
  MONOLINGUAL
     SPANISH
  V  [           ] 2.68            [   ] 0.40
  NV [            ] 2.79           [  ] 0.26

     ENGLISH
  V  [             ] 2.90          [   ] 0.41   *
  NV [     ] 1.66                  [ ] -0.12

  BILINGUAL
     SPANISH
  V  [            ] 2.84           [  ] 0.33
  NV [        ] 2.18               [  ] 0.25

     ENGLISH
  V  [          ] 2.56             [  ] 0.38
  NV [      ] 1.98                 [  ] 0.23

     KEY
       V=VIEWERS
     NV=NONVIEWERS
       * =SIGNIFICANT DIFFERENCE (P<.05)
```

60

FIGURE 4.1 (Continued)

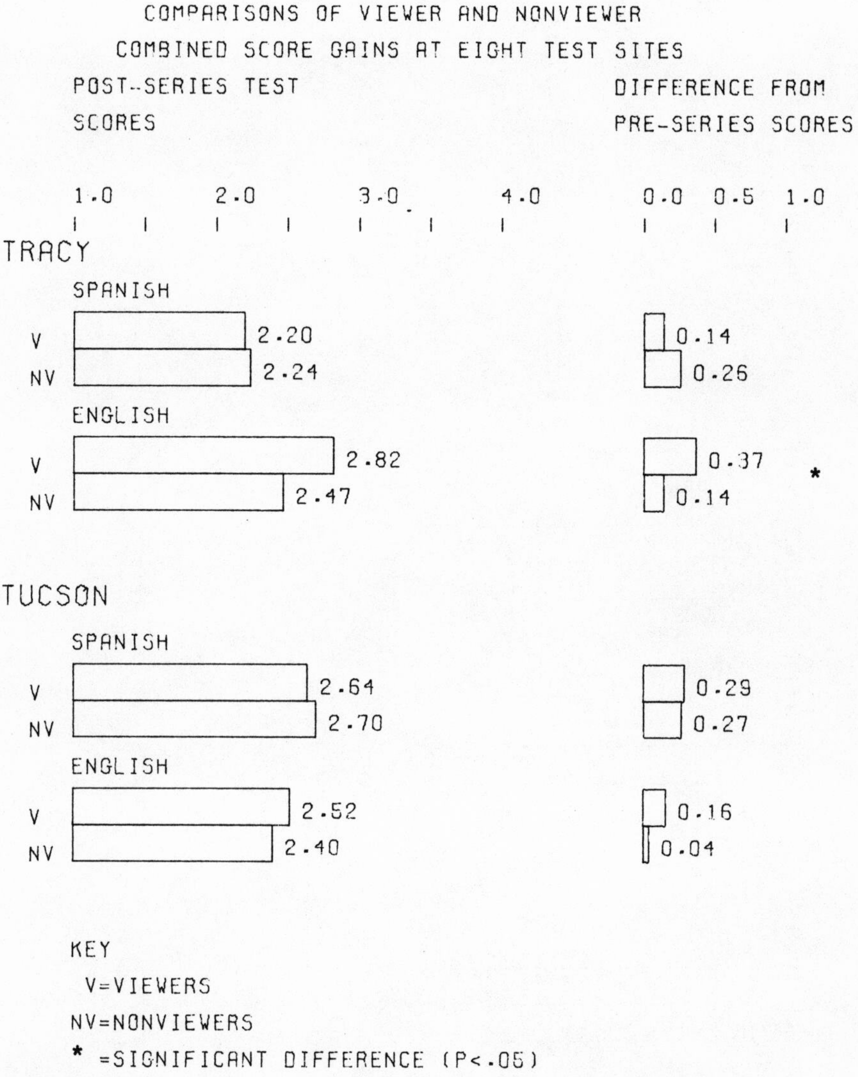

COMPARISONS OF VIEWER AND NONVIEWER
COMBINED SCORE GAINS AT EIGHT TEST SITES

KEY
 V=VIEWERS
NV=NONVIEWERS
 * =SIGNIFICANT DIFFERENCE (P<.05)

FIGURE 4.2

AVERAGE SCORES OF TEST SITES COMBINE

TOTAL

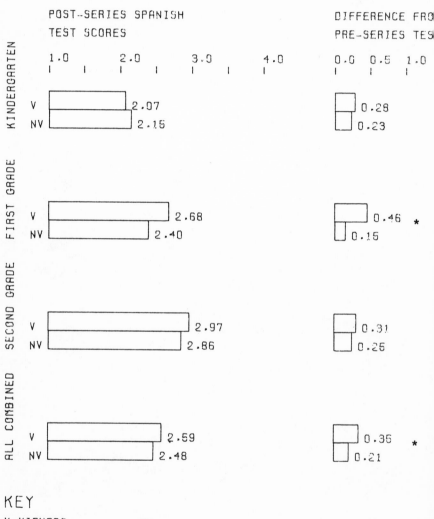

KEY
V=VIEWERS
NV=NONVIEWERS
*=SIGNIFICANT DIFFERENCE (P<.05)

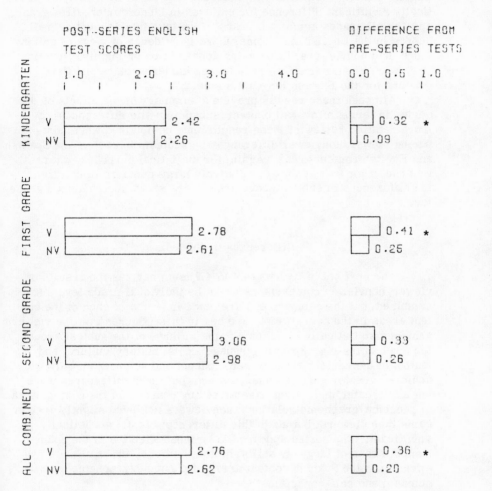

FIGURE 4.3
AVERAGE SCORES OF TEST SITES COMBINED

TOTAL

POST-SERIES ENGLISH
TEST SCORES

DIFFERENCE FROM
PRE-SERIES TESTS

KINDERGARTEN

V 2.42
NV 2.26

0.32 *
0.09

FIRST GRADE

V 2.78
NV 2.61

0.41 *
0.25

SECOND GRADE

V 3.06
NV 2.98

0.33
0.26

ALL COMBINED

V 2.76
NV 2.62

0.36 *
0.20

KEY
V=VIEWERS
NV=NONVIEWERS
*=SIGNIFICANT DIFFERENCE (P<.05)

Thus, while the overall results show that the series had an impact, considering all items in the Spanish area, this was mainly concentrated at the first-grade level.

Figure 4.3 represents a summary of the test averages for English items. Viewer scores exceeded nonviewer scores by a statistically significant difference for children in kindergarten, first grade, and for all grades combined. Thus, if we take into account overall scores in the English test items, there is evidence of viewers gaining more than nonviewers; these gains appear to be primarily a function of viewer/nonviewer differences among kindergartners and first graders for the English language items.

Although these results provide a summary of the effects of the series in terms of overall content (subsuming site differences), a more detailed review of these results may be obtained when comparing viewer/nonviewer differences by subtests in each of the Spanish and English content areas. Again, for statistical purposes, where it was useful for us to compare relatively large numbers of children, the differences in subtest score areas were shown for combined grade levels.

Differences by Subtests

The next set of figures (4.4 to 4.9) summarizes the results of viewer/nonviewer comparisons when the individual grade levels are combined, but the comparisons are made in terms of each of the content areas in the overall test. We see in these figures that the viewers achieved statistically significant gains in three of the subtest areas for Spanish testing: Spanish language skills, history/culture, and math. In the content areas of self-concept and science, viewers achieved greater gains than nonviewers, but these differences were not any greater than might have arisen by chance. In the content area of phoneme/grapheme relations, nonviewers achieved slightly greater gains than viewers, but again this difference was not statistically significant. The series appeared to be most effective in the Spanish content areas of language skills, history/culture, and math, and least effective in the Spanish content areas of phoneme/grapheme relations, science, and self-concept.

Where viewers and nonviewers are compared by grade level, as shown in the accompanying figures, the results indicate greater gain effects for first-grade viewers in four of the six Spanish content areas. These were self-concept, Spanish language skills, history/ culture, and math. Viewers in kindergarten and second grade also showed selected significant gains over nonviewers, but only in the area of history/culture. There was no evidence on any grade level that

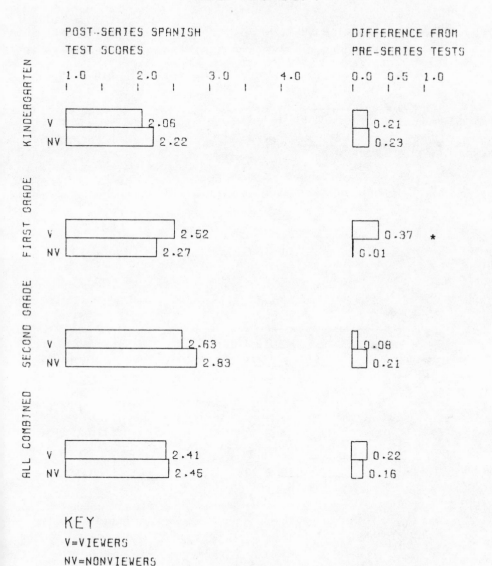

FIGURE 4.4

AVERAGE SCORES OF TEST SITES COMBINED

SELF CONCEPT

POST-SERIES SPANISH
TEST SCORES

DIFFERENCE FROM
PRE-SERIES TESTS

KINDERGARTEN

1.0   2.0   3.0   4.0

0.0 0.5 1.0

V — 2.06
NV — 2.22

0.21
0.23

FIRST GRADE

V — 2.52
NV — 2.27

0.37 *
0.01

SECOND GRADE

V — 2.63
NV — 2.83

0.08
0.21

ALL COMBINED

V — 2.41
NV — 2.45

0.22
0.16

KEY
V=VIEWERS
NV=NONVIEWERS
*=SIGNIFICANT DIFFERENCE (P<.05)

FIGURE 4.5

AVERAGE SCORES OF TEST SITES COMBINED

SPANISH

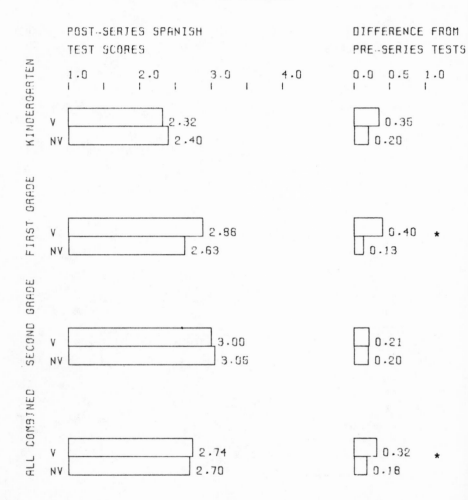

KEY

V=VIEWERS

NV=NONVIEWERS

*=SIGNIFICANT DIFFERENCE (P<.05)

FIGURE 4.6

AVERAGE SCORES OF TEST SITES COMBINED

HISTORY CULTURE

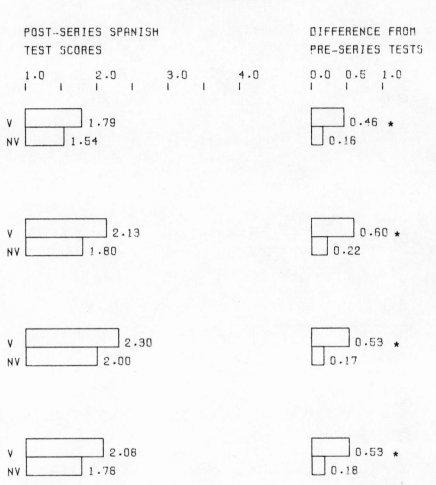

POST-SERIES SPANISH
TEST SCORES

DIFFERENCE FROM
PRE-SERIES TESTS

KINDERGARTEN

V 1.79
NV 1.54

0.46 *
0.16

FIRST GRADE

V 2.13
NV 1.80

0.60 *
0.22

SECOND GRADE

V 2.30
NV 2.00

0.53 *
0.17

ALL COMBINED

V 2.08
NV 1.78

0.53 *
0.18

KEY
V=VIEWERS
NV=NONVIEWERS
*=SIGNIFICANT DIFFERENCE (P<.05)

FIGURE 4.7

AVERAGE SCORES OF TEST SITES COMBINE

SCIENCE

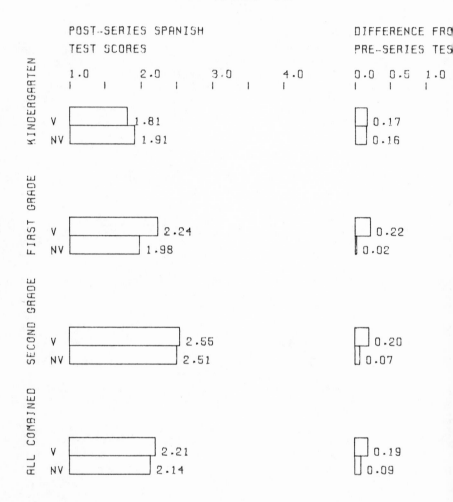

POST-SERIES SPANISH
TEST SCORES

DIFFERENCE FRO
PRE-SERIES TES

KINDERGARTEN
V 1.81
NV 1.91
0.17
0.16

FIRST GRADE
V 2.24
NV 1.98
0.22
0.02

SECOND GRADE
V 2.55
NV 2.51
0.20
0.07

ALL COMBINED
V 2.21
NV 2.14
0.19
0.09

KEY
V=VIEWERS
NV=NONVIEWERS
*=SIGNIFICANT DIFFERENCE (P<.05)

FIGURE 4.8

AVERAGE SCORES OF TEST SITES COMBINED

PHONEME/GRAPHEME

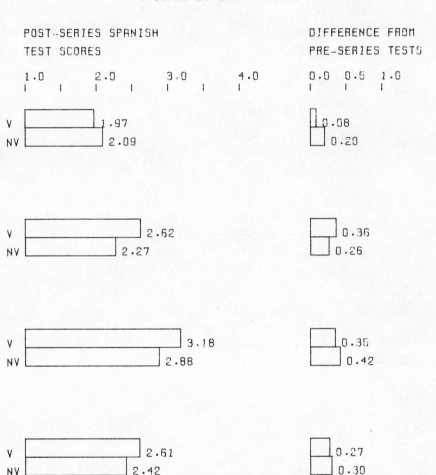

POST-SERIES SPANISH
TEST SCORES

DIFFERENCE FROM
PRE-SERIES TESTS

KINDERGARTEN

V .97
NV 2.09

0.08
0.20

FIRST GRADE

V 2.62
NV 2.27

0.36
0.26

SECOND GRADE

V 3.18
NV 2.88

0.35
0.42

ALL COMBINED

V 2.61
NV 2.42

0.27
0.30

KEY

V=VIEWERS

NV=NONVIEWERS

=SIGNIFICANT DIFFERENCE (P<.05)

FIGURE 4.9

AVERAGE SCORES OF TEST SITES COMBINED

MATH

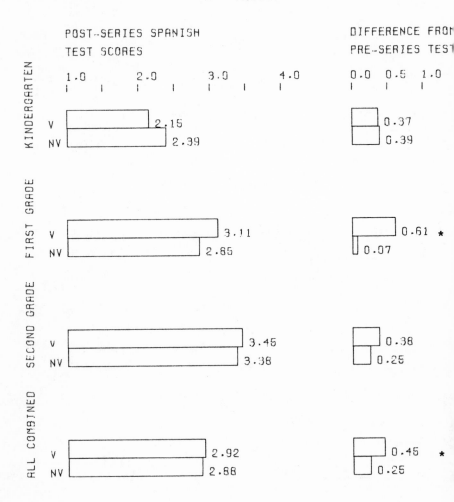

KEY

V=VIEWERS

NV=NONVIEWERS

*=SIGNIFICANT DIFFERENCE (P<.05)

FIGURE 4.10

AVERAGE SCORES OF TEST SITES COMBINED

SELF CONCEPT

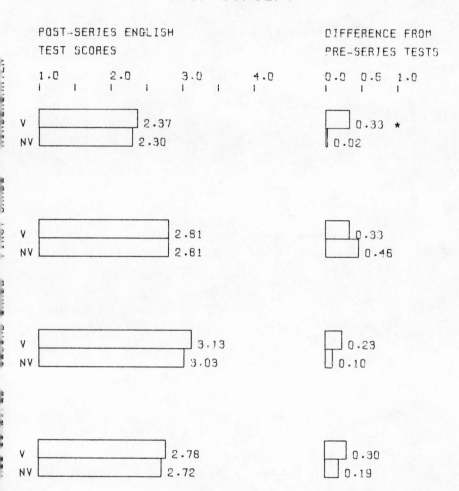

POST-SERIES ENGLISH TEST SCORES

| 1.0 | 2.0 | 3.0 | 4.0 |

V 2.37
NV 2.30

DIFFERENCE FROM PRE-SERIES TESTS

| 0.0 | 0.5 | 1.0 |

0.33 *
0.02

V 2.81
NV 2.81

0.33
0.46

V 3.13
NV 3.03

0.23
0.10

V 2.78
NV 2.72

0.30
0.19

EY
=VIEWERS
=NONVIEWERS
=SIGNIFICANT DIFFERENCE (P<.05)

FIGURE 4.11

AVERAGE SCORES OF TEST SITES COMBIN

ENGLISH

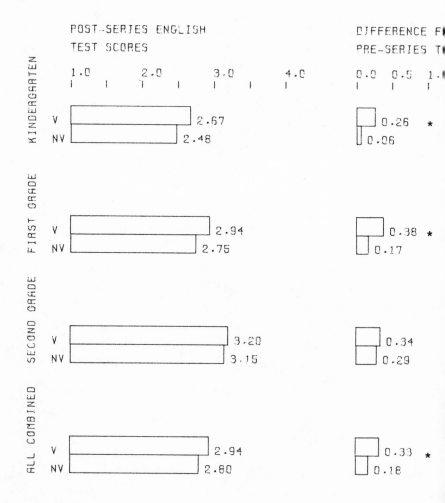

KEY
V=VIEWERS
NV=NONVIEWERS
*=SIGNIFICANT DIFFERENCE (P<.05)

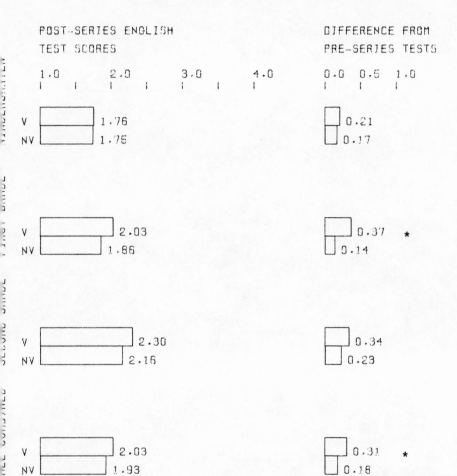

FIGURE 4.12
AVERAGE SCORES OF TEST SITES COMBINED

HISTORY CULTURE

POST-SERIES ENGLISH
TEST SCORES

DIFFERENCE FROM
PRE-SERIES TESTS

```
1.0       2.0       3.0       4.0      0.0  0.5  1.0
```

V   1.76
NV   1.75

0.21
0.17

V   2.03
NV   1.86

0.37 *
0.14

V   2.30
NV   2.16

0.34
0.23

V   2.03
NV   1.93

0.31 *
0.18

KEY
V=VIEWERS
NV=NONVIEWERS
*=SIGNIFICANT DIFFERENCE (P<.05)

73

FIGURE 4.13

AVERAGE SCORES OF TEST SITES COMBIN

SCIENCE

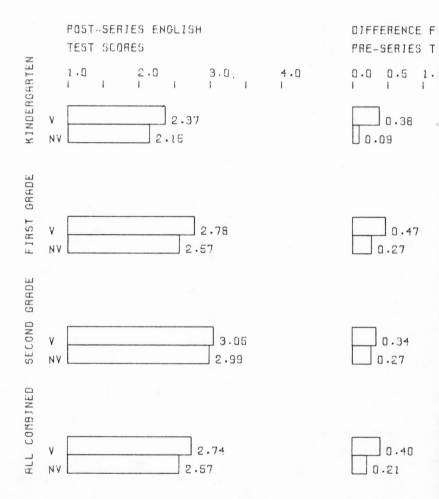

POST-SERIES ENGLISH
TEST SCORES

DIFFERENCE F
PRE-SERIES T

KINDERGARTEN

V 2.37
NV 2.15

0.38
0.09

FIRST GRADE

V 2.78
NV 2.57

0.47
0.27

SECOND GRADE

V 3.05
NV 2.99

0.34
0.27

ALL COMBINED

V 2.74
NV 2.57

0.40
0.21

KEY
V=VIEWERS
NV=NONVIEWERS
*=SIGNIFICANT DIFFERENCE (P<.05)

viewers exceeded nonviewers in the areas of phoneme/grapheme relations or science.

Similar to the comparisons of differences between viewers and nonviewers in each of the content areas of the Spanish testing, Figures 4.10 to 4.13 summarize these comparisons in the English testing areas. We see here that viewers achieved significantly greater gains than nonviewers in the three areas of English language skills, history/culture, and science. Although the average gain of viewers was greater than that of nonviewers in the area of self-concept, we could have little confidence that this difference was due to more than chance.

The most general conclusion, then, was that in the English content areas, the effect of the series was most pronounced in terms of English language skills, history/culture, and science. By contrast, the series appeared to have no more than a chance effect in the English content area of self-concept.

When comparisons were made between viewers and nonviewers in each grade level, as in the accompanying figures, viewers in the kindergarten level achieved significantly greater gains over nonviewers in three of the four content areas: self-concept, English language skills, and science. First-grade viewers exceeded nonviewers in the areas of English language skills and history/culture. Although first-grade viewers tended to exceed nonviewers at a level just short of statistical significance in science, we cannot have confidence in this effect. It is noteworthy that no significant effects were found in any of the subtest areas for second graders.

Fluency ratings assigned by the interviewers during the tests were measured on a 1-4 scale as previously discussed in Chapter 3. Figures 4.14 and 4.15 present the average fluency of all viewer/non-viewer groups in Spanish and English. Gains in fluency achieved statistical significance for second-grade viewers in English, and no other fluency gains in either Spanish or English were significant.

SOME GENERALIZATIONS

In this chapter we have seen the national test results in terms of a number of different contrasts when viewers and nonviewers are compared. One of these was in the different sites where overall viewer/nonviewer comparisons were made. Results indicated evidence of the impact of the program upon viewers, but this was divided across sites and across the Spanish and English areas with no major evident pattern. In other comparisons, subtests were investigated, but in terms of test sites combined. Here the results indicated a consistent pattern of effects for kindergartners, particularly in most of the Spanish testing areas, and for kindergartners and first graders,

FIGURE 4.14

AVERAGE SCORES OF TEST SITES COMBINE

FLUENCY

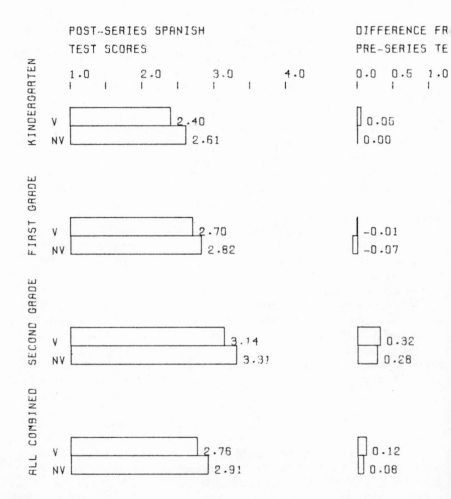

KEY
V=VIEWERS
NV=NONVIEWERS
*=SIGNIFICANT DIFFERENCE (P<.05)

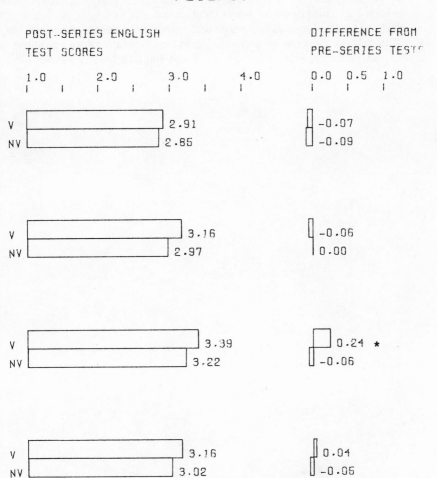

FIGURE 4.15

AVERAGE SCORES OF TEST SITES COMBINED

FLUENCY

POST-SERIES ENGLISH TEST SCORES

DIFFERENCE FROM PRE-SERIES TEST

KINDERGARTEN

V 2.91 −0.07
NV 2.85 −0.09

FIRST GRADE

V 3.16 −0.06
NV 2.97 0.00

SECOND GRADE

V 3.39 0.24 *
NV 3.22 −0.06

ALL COMBINED

V 3.16 0.04
NV 3.02 −0.05

KEY
V=VIEWERS
NV=NONVIEWERS
*=SIGNIFICANT DIFFERENCE (P<.05)

77

particularly in most of the English testing areas. Thus, the program had more effect on kindergartners and first graders in the Spanish and English areas than it did on second graders. An examination of the pretest scores indicate that second graders tend to have a more advanced preseries knowledge of the materials and thus do not gain, relative to kindergartners and first graders. Further, it seems clear that certain subtest areas show no impact as a result of the series. This was in the area of phoneme/grapheme relations and science in Spanish testing, and self-concept in the English testing area.

5

Other than directly testing the effects of the program on the children, information gained from teachers was probably the second best source of evaluation of "Carrascolendas." This information was gained in two ways. One was to ask teachers to keep a fairly complete program-by-program diary of the entire series; another was to have teachers fill out a relatively simple questionnaire (averaging about 39 questions) concerning a variety of facets of the series. This chapter is a summary and interpretation of the questionnaire results for the three years. The diary results are the topic of Chapter 6.

THE QUESTIONNAIRE AND ITS DISTRIBUTION

The basic design of the questionnaire was of necessity a compromise between the information we wanted about the series and the information teachers would willingly and reliably provide. It was decided to keep the questionnaire short, about two to three pages, to enhance the percentage of questionnaires returned. The questionnaire for the first year was drafted and pilot tested on a small group of teachers before final editing and distribution. The format of the questionnaire was kept simple, so the teachers could easily check off answers. The questionnaire for the second year was revised to exclude questions from the first year that did not yield useful information. Other questions were added, but the total was kept to 43 questions. For the third year, the questionnaire was revised to reflect a national mailing. For example, information on the different types of viewing sites was included. A copy of the third-year questionnaire is reproduced in Appendix C.

In each of the three years, the dissemination of questionnaires was the same. In an initial phase of the survey work on the project, a very brief postcard inquiry was sent to schools thought likely to be users of the series. In the first two years these were schools located in Texas; in the third year the usage questionnaire was sent to schools in the United States where Spanish-surnamed students are at least 10 percent of the school population. More details of the usage survey may be found in Chapter 8. Most of the questions on the usage survey concerned the estimation of the number of classes that would be viewing "Carrascolendas." Schools that returned the postcard indicated usage of the series in a particular number of classes. This number of teacher questionnaires was then sent to the principal with an accompanying letter requesting that they be distributed and returned in enclosed envelopes to the researchers. A sample of the letter for the third year may be found along with the questionnaire in Appendix C.

In the first year the majority of questionnaires returned came from the central Texas areas in and around San Antonio and Austin respectively. The second and third years in Texas had returns similar to the first, but indicated increased response from the Lower Rio Grande Valley, which has a large Mexican-American population. In the national study more than two-thirds of the responses came from Texas; the remainder were concentrated in California, New Mexico, and Colorado.

To provide the clearest overview of the type of information obtained from the questionnaires, questions from all three surveys are clustered into selected content areas, and their results are summarized across the number of years in which the questions were used. The column headed "National" excludes the data from Texas for that year.

PUPIL CHARACTERISTICS

Most classrooms were predominantly made up of Mexican-American students, a large percentage of whom spoke Spanish. In the third year of the survey the teachers were asked to rate the Mexican-American children in terms of the children's self-esteem. In both the Texas and remaining national data the categories of "feeling proud" or "accepting one's heritage" represented the majority of responses. One-third of the responses in the Texas data and about one-fourth in the national data showed that the Mexican-American children had no awareness of differences between their heritage and any other ethnic group. Questions and results disclosing pupil characteristics were as follows:

What is the approximate percentage of the ethnic groups
represented in your class?

Responses	Texas (N = 196) March 1971	Texas (N = 163) March 1972	Texas (N = 290) Nov. 1972	National (N = 86) Nov. 1972
Mexican-American	76%	78%	84%	60%
Black	6	5	4	4
Anglo	18	12	11	30
Other	0	5	1	6

What percentage of the children in your class
speak Spanish?

Texas (N = 196) March 1971	Texas (N = 163) March 1972	Texas (N = 290) Nov. 1972	National (N = 86) Nov. 1972
75%	77%	84%	60%

In general, how would you rate the Mexican-American
children's self-esteem in your classrooms?

Responses	Texas (N = 290) Nov. 1972	National (N = 86) Nov. 1972
High, proud of his Mexican-American heritage	26%	35%
Medium, accepts his heritage	37	35
Low, embarrassed by his heritage	1	2
No awareness of difference between Mexican-American heritage and any other ethnic group	35	22
No Mexican-American children present	0	4
No response	1	2

TEACHERS' LANGUAGE ABILITY

Despite the fact that three-fourths of the students in the classrooms surveyed spoke Spanish, many of the teachers rated their
Spanish as limited or indicated that they spoke English only. In the
second- and third-year evaluation nearly one-third of the teachers
indicated that they spoke Spanish fluently.

81

How well do you speak Spanish?

Responses	Texas (N = 196) March 1971	Texas (N = 163) March 1972	Texas (N = 290) Nov. 1972	National (N = 86) Nov. 1972
Fluently	30%	29%	33%	30%
Moderately	15	23	17	15
Limitedly	32	25	31	22
English only	23	23	19	33

PUBLICITY

As will be noted in Chapter 8, the usage survey indicated that one major shortcoming was the dissemination of information about the availability of the program. Accordingly, it was interesting to find out whether teachers were aware of any publicity regarding the program. Questionnaire results indicated that most publicity was found in newspapers. Also, during the third year, teachers were asked if they were aware of any other bilingual children's television program; generally they were not.

Has there been any publicity regarding "Carrascolendas" in your area?

Responses	Texas (N = 290) Nov. 1972	National (N = 86) Nov. 1972
Yes, newspaper	33%	23%
Yes, television or radio	13	8
Yes, national publication	0	2
Yes, local publication	18	11
None	30	50
No response	6	6

Have you heard of any other bilingual children's television programs?

Responses	Texas (N = 290) Nov. 1972	National (N = 86) Nov. 1972
No	88%	76%
Yes	12	24

Responses	Texas (N=290) Nov. 1972	National (N=86) Nov. 1972
If yes, percentage also mentioning "Sesame Street"	4	7

VIEWING SITUATION

In the first year's survey, teachers were asked several questions about when they would like to have the series presented. Fifty percent preferred the fall and 31 percent preferred the spring. Teachers tended to favor the program being shown three days a week (57 percent) and were almost evenly divided as to whether to show the program during morning hours (45 percent) or afternoon (43 percent). Some 42 percent said that if the program were to be repeated outside of school hours it should come on Saturday morning and 30 percent suggested weekdays after school.

Questions pertaining to viewing circumstances in the schools indicated that an average of 32 children were gathered together to view a single set, that most children see programs three times a week, that the television reception was always or often satisfactory, and that most watched the series in black and white.

Approximately how many students watch the same television set?

Texas (N=196) March 1971	Texas (N=290) Nov. 1972	National (N=86) Nov. 1972
Average = 32	Average = 47	Average = 35

How often does your class watch "Carrascolendas?"

Responses	Texas (N=196) March 1971	Texas (N=163) March 1972	Texas (N=290) Nov. 1972	National (N=86) Nov. 1972
Every program	83%	81%	62%	60%
Twice a week	8	12	10	20
Once a week	5	4	23	14
Less than once a week	4	1	3	5

Responses	Texas (N = 196) March 1971	Texas (N = 163) March 1972	Texas (N = 290) Nov. 1972	National (N = 86) Nov. 1972
Never	0	1	1	0
No response	0	1	1	1

Is your television reception of "Carrascolendas" satisfactory?

Responses	Texas (N = 196) March 1971	Texas (N = 163) March 1972	Texas (N = 290) Nov. 1972	National (N = 86) Nov. 1972
Always	41%	53%	39%	50%
Often	43	40	44	41
Rarely	13	6	14	6
Never	2	0	2	1
No response	1	1	1	2

Do you watch the program in color?

Responses	Texas (N = 163) March 1972	Texas (N = 290) Nov. 1972	National (N = 86) Nov. 1972
Yes	6%	19%	2%
No, black and white	93	79	97
No response	1	2	1

TEACHER-INITIATED CLASS ACTIVITIES

As to the frequency with which teachers directly conducted related classroom activities, most teachers' responses were divided between categories of "often" and "rarely." There was further indication that such activities were rarely conducted solely in Spanish, but mostly in English or in a mixture of Spanish and English. Finally, results indicated that when activities were offered, most Mexican-American children engaged in them. The results of a question not summarized here indicated that most teachers either conducted activities after the program or a mixture of before and after, but very few teachers conducted activities only before the children saw the program.

Do you conduct any class activities about "Carrascolendas"
before or after viewing the program?

Responses	Texas (N = 196) March 1971	Texas (N = 163) March 1972	Texas (N = 290) Nov. 1972	National (N = 86) Nov. 1972
Always	0%	5%	8%	6%
Often	59	34	39	34
Rarely	27	32	35	42
Never	9	26	11	16
No response	5	3	7	2

Are class activities prior to viewing "Carrascolendas"
conducted in Spanish or English?

Responses	Texas (N = 163) March 1972	Texas (N = 290) Nov. 1972	National (N = 86) Nov. 1972
Mostly in Spanish	7%	4%	5%
Mostly in English	52	63	68
Mostly half and half	20	28	22
No previewing activities	18	4	5
No response	3	1	0

Do the Mexican-American children in your class
participate in class activities?

Responses	Texas (N = 163) March 1972	Texas (N = 290) Nov. 1972	National (N = 86) Nov. 1972
Very much	73%	75%	62%
Moderately	23	20	23
A little	3	3	8
Not at all	0	0	0
No responses	1	2	7

PARTICIPATION OF MEXICAN-AMERICAN CHILDREN

As described in Chapter 2, a number of the segments in a typical
"Carrascolendas" program involved materials that would invite a

85

child's active participation. Teachers were asked to gauge such participation either as they observed it in a direct response to the viewing segment of the program or as a kind of aftereffect of viewing the program. In their response to questions not summarized here, the results of the first two years indicated that teachers generally rated class participation in these segments as occurring "all the time" or at least "often."

Do Spanish-speaking children engage in the Spanish and/or English audience participation segments during the program?

Responses	Texas (N= 196) March 1971		Texas (N = 290) Nov. 1972		National (N = 86) Nov. 1972	
	Spanish	English	Spanish	English	Spanish	English
Most engaged all of the time	42%	38%	48%	24%	40%	22%
Most engaged some of the time	31	33	39	31	40	30
A few engaged most of the time	11	7	5	5	7	10
A few engaged some of the time	7	6	3	6	6	12
Little participation	2	1	1	5	3	8
No response	7	15	4	29	4	18

Are Mexican-American children willing to contribute experiences from their backgrounds during discussions pertaining to "Carrascolendas?"

Responses	Texas (N = 196) March 1971	Texas (N = 163) March 1972	Texas (N = 290) Nov. 1972	National (N = 86) Nov. 1972
Yes, often	} 67%	32%	36%	29%
Yes, occasionally		49	51	52
No, never	19	16	9	10
No response	14	3	4	9

PARTICIPATION OF OTHER CHILDREN

Although the primary target audience of "Carrascolendas" is Mexican-American, it is important to know the responses of children in other ethnic groups and how the program may promote cultural interchange of these children with the Mexican-American children. Results indicated a generally favorable response by the non-Mexican-American children to the program, as well as some evidence of exchange of cultural information among the children. Additionally, teachers indicated that they generally explained Spanish segments to non-Spanish-speaking children.

Do English-speaking children engage in the Spanish and/or English audience participation segments during the program?

Responses	Texas (N = 163) March 1972 Spanish	English	Texas (N = 290) Nov. 1972 Spanish	English	National (N = 86) Nov. 1972 Spanish	English
Most engaged all of the time	24%	33%	37%	30%	41%	42%
Most engaged some of the time	26	25	35	26	34	27
A few engaged most of the time	7	5	8	5	4	5
A few engaged some of the time	9	5	7	5	6	6
Little participation	6	3	3	5	4	3
No response	28	29	10	29	11	17

Have non-Spanish speakers learned some Spanish after watching the program?

Responses	Texas (N = 196) March 1971	Texas (N = 163) March 1972	Texas (N = 290) Nov. 1972	National (N = 86) Nov. 1972
Some Spanish	} 40%	24%	23%	40%
A little Spanish		38	42	43
No Spanish	2	5	4	6

87

	Texas (N = 196) March 1971	Texas (N = 163) March 1972	Texas (N = 290) Nov. 1972	National (N = 86) Nov. 1972
Responses				
No response or no non-Spanish speakers present	58	33	31	11

Do non-Spanish-speaking students ask the Mexican-American children about "Carrascolendas?"

	Texas (N = 163) March 1972	Texas (N = 290) Nov. 1972	National (N = 86) Nov. 1972
Responses			
Yes, often	4%	10%	16%
Yes, occasionally	29	31	47
No, never	25	19	26
No response or no non-Spanish speakers present	42	40	11

Have children from other ethnic groups shown interest in learning more about Mexican culture after watching "Carrascolendas?"

	Texas (N = 196) March 1971	Texas (N = 163) March 1972	Texas (N = 290) Nov. 1972	National (N =86) Nov. 1972
Responses				
Yes often }	11%	6%	9%	22%
Yes, occasionally }		28	31	53
No, never	26	18	13	8
No response or no other ethnic groups present	63	48	47	17

How do you explain the Spanish segments to
non-Spanish-speaking students?

Responses	Texas (N = 196) March 1971	Texas (N = 163) March 1972	Texas (N=290) Nov. 1972	National (N = 86) Nov. 1972
You explain in English	23%	41%	32%	48%
Aide or parent explains	2	2	5	5
Spanish-speaking student explains	15	10	13	11
No explanations are made	9	11	16	21
No response or non-Spanish speakers present	51	36	34	15

APPROPRIATENESS

Several questions used during the three years asked teachers
to evaluate the appropriateness of the level of the instructional materials in the series. For the most part, responses were favorable.
This included the evaluation of the language levels of English and
Spanish used in the series. In the results of the first year's evaluation, the appropriateness of the instructional level of "Carrascolendas"
was rated as follows: "always" (21 percent), "almost always" (60
percent), "sometimes" (14 percent), "never" (1 percent), and "no
response" (4 percent). More detailed questions were posed in the
subsequent versions of the questionnaire.

Is the subject content of "Carrascolendas" appropriate
for your students?

Subject Area	Responses	Texas (N = 163) March 1972	Texas (N=290) Nov. 1972	National (N=86) Nov. 1972
Math	Always	37%	34%	31%
	Often	40	48	47
	Rarely	17	12	12
	Never	1	1	3
	No response	5	5	7

Subject Area	Responses	Texas (N = 163) March 1972	Texas (N = 290) Nov. 1972	National (N = 86) Nov. 1972
Science	Always	35%	22%	20%
	Often	40	42	49
	Rarely	7	24	20
	Never	3	3	3
	No response	15	9	8
Spanish	Always	59%	55%	29%
	Often	30	36	49
	Rarely	4	4	15
	Never	1	1	3
	No response	6	4	4
English	Always	56%	42%	43%
	Often	33	43	49
	Rarely	6	8	4
	Never	0	0	2
	No response	5	7	2

Is the language level of "Carrascolendas" appropriate
for your students' understanding?

Responses	Texas (N = 163) March 1972		Texas (N = 290) Nov. 1972		National (N = 86) Nov. 1972	
	Spanish	English	Spanish	English	Spanish	English
Always	50%	52%	45%	40%	36%	44%
Often	36	31	48	43	37	43
Rarely	7	3	3	8	22	6
Never	0	0	1	0	2	1
No response	7	14	3	9	3	6

Was the cultural and historical content beneficial
for your students?

Responses	Texas (N = 163) March 1972	Texas (N = 290) Nov. 1972	Texas (N = 86) Nov. 1972
Very much	48%	38%	41%
Somewhat	39	39	39
A little	6	16	14
Not at all	3	3	0
No response	4	4	6

How valuable were the animation segments presenting
letter/sound relationships?

Responses	Texas (N = 163) March 1972	Texas (N=290) Nov. 1972	National (N=86) Nov. 1972
Very valuable	62%	58%	64%
Somewhat valuable	26	32	29
A little valuable	9	6	5
Of no value	1	1	0
No response	2	3	2

EFFECTS ON SELF-CONCEPT

A variety of questions over the three years asked the teachers
to evaluate various consequences of the program. One such question
during the first year asked the teacher whether she felt more confident
in a bilingual classroom as a result of watching this program. Some
64 percent of the teachers responded positively. Another productive
question in the first year's evaluation was "What was the most significant effect of the program?" Responses were as follows:

	(N=259)
Spanish children show self concept improvement	18%
Children interested in learning Spanish	17%
Children entertained by program	15%
Spanish children and culture gain more respect from others	10%
Spanish children more at ease with speaking Spanish	9%
Spanish children more aware of their culture	5%
Miscellaneous comments	4%
Reinforced school curriculum	3%
No response	19%

This was followed in the subsequent questionnaires by a question
that focused directly on teachers' impressions of Mexican-American
children's self-esteem.

Do you think that the Mexican-American children's
self-esteem or pride may benefit from watching
"Carrascolendas?"

Responses	Texas (N = 290) Nov. 1972	National (N = 86) Nov. 1972
Very much	49%	57%
Moderately	28	23
A little	15	12
Not at all	5	3
No response or no Mexican-American children present	3	5

FREQUENCY OF SPANISH USAGE

Regarding the effects of "Carrascolendas" in encouraging the
children's use of Spanish, the following question showed mixed responses between "no effect" and "somewhat."

Do Mexican-American children speak Spanish in school
more often after watching the program?

Responses	Texas (N=196) March 1972	Texas (N=290) Nov. 1972	National (N=86) Nov. 1972
Yes, often	8%	17%	16%
Yes, somewhat	36	38	31
No, not at all	49	40	42
No response or no Mexican-American children present	7	5	11

POPULARITY OF THE SERIES

In each year of the survey there was a question about the popu-
larity of the series. Responses indicated that teachers thought children liked "Carrascolendas" "very much."

In general, how well do you think your students
like "Carrascolendas?"

Responses	Texas (N = 196) March 1971	Texas (N = 163) March 1972	Texas (N = 290) Nov. 1972	National (N = 86) Nov. 1972
Very much	79%	76%	75%	63%
Moderately	0	23	19	30
A little	19	0	3	5
Not at all	1	0	1	0
No response	1	1	2	2

Would you like to see the series repeated next year?

Responses	Texas (N = 196) March 1971	Texas (N = 163) March 1972	Texas (N = 290) Nov. 1972	National (N = 86) Nov. 1972
Yes	83%	87%	89%	80%
No	8	3	2	11
No opinion	9	6	7	8
No response	0	4	2	1

Would you like to see a follow-up program for your
students at a more advanced level next year?

Responses	Texas (N = 196) March 1971	Texas (N = 163) March 1972	Texas (N = 290) Nov. 1972	National (N = 86) Nov. 1972
Yes	80%	69%	56%	51%
No	4	18	26	33
No opinion or no response	16	13	18	16

IMPRESSIONS OF SIGNIFICANT EFFECTS

Eighty-eight percent of the respondents to the Teacher Attitude
Questionnaire replied to its one open-ended question: "What do you
think is the most significant effect of "Carrascolendas" on your
students?" The gist of those comments mentioned most often were:

1. Mexican-American children indicate increased pride in
their language and culture when they hear their language used on
television.

93

2. "Carrascolendas" had the effect of increasing vocabularies in both Spanish and English.

3. Cultural and ethnic differences are better understood and appreciated after viewing the series.

4. "Carrascolendas" is enjoyable and entertaining—particularly the songs, which permit much audience participation, and the characters, riddles, rhymes, and games.

5. Children evidence increased self-esteem; the Spanish-speaking children participate more and volunteer more information in class.

SUMMARY

The following generalizations can be derived from the Teacher Attitude Questionnaire response data:

1. A high proportion of Mexican-American children felt proud or at least accepting of their cultural heritage; the program was thought to increase self-esteem.

2. The program was very popular with teachers and children; animation was highly rated for entertainment value and as an instructional technique.

3. There was active participation in the program on the part of English-speaking children who benefited by learning some Spanish and by becoming interested in another culture.

4. In the four main subject areas—math, science, Spanish, and English—the level of material presented was judged by the majority of teachers to be always, or often, appropriate for their students. The Texas results showed particularly high percentages.

6

TEACHERS'
EVALUATIONS

As mentioned at the outset of the last chapter, we considered teachers' evaluations to be the second best source of assessment of the program, compared with direct testing of the children. In addition to questionnaires, our second type of teacher evaluation, the topic of this chapter, involved evaluations gathered on a program-by-program basis. For the duration of the project, we have referred to these materials as the "Teacher Diaries."

In our first year's evaluation, teachers in bilingual programs in the Austin, Texas area were given small notebooks containing a page for each program. Teachers were asked to comment on each of the 30 programs in the first year's series. In the second and third years the observation notebooks were replaced by Teacher Diaries in which the teachers could continue their role of viewer-critic for each program. In the second year we distributed diaries to teachers throughout Texas. They consisted of a three-part evaluation sheet for each program. In the final year, to insure completeness of individual diaries and adequate numbers for analysis from different test sites, we contracted and paid selected teachers at each test site to keep diaries.

THE FIRST YEAR: OBSERVATION NOTEBOOKS

Diaries prepared during the first year contained 30 pages; each page was dated for a particular broadcast day. Teachers were asked to jot down comments concerning program content, objectives, format, children's reactions, their own personal reactions, notes on linguistic usage, and comments about television reception. In short, we encouraged teachers to record any comment that seemed important to them. These notebooks were distributed to 90 teachers in the Austin, Texas area prior to the first program in the series on February 15, 1970. Forty-three notebooks were collected after the final program

(May 3), and their comments were tabulated and summarized. Summaries were done by selecting quotations from the notebooks and paraphrasing them on a program-by-program basis. For example, this is the summary for Program 5 broadcast on February 24:

Teachers were very enthusiastic about the dramatization "dealing with fear." They felt this was a very important concept for the children to explore. They reported that the students watched this segment unusually attentively and that follow-up in the classroom was quite successful.

The "nonequivalent sets" instruction was not considered successful in that it was too brief and many children did not seem to understand it. It was suggested that objects be used in the demonstration instead of pictures and that more time be spent on equivalent sets before introducing the concept of nonequivalence.

A few teachers reported that the film about corn and tortillas was interesting and led to related classroom activities, but most of the comments indicated that the film did not include enough action to maintain the interest of the students who were restless and talkative during this portion of the program.

The above was a sample of responses collated for a particular program; the following is the summary of comments for the 30 programs presented in the first-year evaluation report:

Almost every teacher commented negatively on the use of cursive writing for the presentation of letters. This departure from their own schoolroom practice was thought to be confusing to the students.

There were differences of opinion regarding the format of "Carrascolendas." Some teachers felt there were too many segments that were too short and that the programs needed sequence; others felt that the fast pace was essential to maintain interest.

The use and treatment of Spanish and English brought a wide variety of opinion. Some felt that vocabulary drill, sentence repetition, and translation aloud from one language to the other needed emphasis. Some felt that all Spanish dramatizations were very effective in encouraging bilingualism, while others were quite frustrated by the use of any extended sequence of Spanish language.

Many teachers commented that the songs were too fast; they suggested that the children have more instruction in the words to songs, with more opportunity for singing along with the television characters. Some kind of intermission or "stretch break" was suggested by teachers who indicated that 30 minutes was too long a period for children of this age.

A number of teachers suggested scheduling the series during the afternoon. Early lunch in elementary schools, free-choice periods, reading groups, and structured morning lessons were all cited as problems with a morning time slot.

THE SECOND YEAR: TEACHER RATINGS

Because the observation notebooks seemed to be too open-ended for some teachers, and because they were difficult to tabulate in a systematic manner, a new type of program diary format was developed for the second year. Among various types of formats that were tried, we found that teachers would readily complete scales of the following type:

THE PROGRAM HELD THE CHILDREN'S INTEREST:

very well (1)___ :___ :___ :___ :___ :___ :___ (7) not at all

Scales developed for the five different aspects of the program are presented in Figure 6.1. Also shown in this figure are questions about the effectiveness of different segments of the program and a space to list further comments.

Return of the second-year diaries was not particularly successful, possibly because they looked as if they were more time consuming than they actually were. Some 500 diaries were sent to teachers who had requested a teacher guide from the Educational Service Center. Only 76 (15 percent) were returned. Of these, 38 percent came from kindergarten teachers, 43 percent from first-grade teachers, and 18 percent from second-grade teachers. All but ten classes were comprised mainly of Mexican-American students; of the ten, nine classes had predominately Anglo and one had predominately black students. Responses were mixed in terms of the amount of Spanish taught in the school; 34 percent of the teachers indicated that about half of their class activities were conducted in Spanish, 28 percent used Spanish less than half of the time, and 21 percent used no Spanish in class. About one-third of the teachers indicated that they spoke no Spanish themselves, while the remainder reported varying degrees of fluency in Spanish.

Average Ratings on the Scales

Results of the ratings for the 30 programs are summarized in Figures 6.2 to 6.7. Each of these figures summarizes the average response of teachers on a particular rating scale. On each figure, averages are presented separately for kindergarten, first, and second grades, and across the 30 programs. Thus, when looking at one of these figures, left-right variations indicate differences among the 30 programs on a program-to-program basis.

Figure 6.2 indicates that the program content was judged slightly less appropriate at the kindergarten level, though the rating never fell below the midpoint. The second-grade level averaged the highest ratings. The content of the last five programs in the series seemed to have been particularly suitable for second graders and least suitable for kindergartners.

In Figure 6.3 it can be seen that the language-level pattern shared its highest ratings between first and second graders. Only for Program 24 did the kindergarten level fall slightly below the midpoint. Programs 3 and 15 were most highly rated for the first-grade level.

Figure 6.4 depicts which programs at which grade level best held the children's interest. Here, the first and second grade shared the highest ratings alternately throughout the series. Again, for Program 24 the kindergarten level was the only one that fell slightly below the midpoint.

In facilitation of learning activities, Figure 6.5, ratings fell to the midpoint for kindergarten or second grade on five programs. On this dimension the first grade seemed to be the most consistently positive throughout the series.

In Figure 6.6, verbal participation was lowest at the kindergarten level for the last several programs of the series. First and second graders participated about equally, but were stimulated by different programs.

Figure 6.7 represents a comparison of each program to the others in the series. Programs 18 and 23 compared least favorably at the kindergarten level. Program 15 had an especially high rating at the first-grade level, as did Program 30 at the second-grade level.

Evaluations of Segment Types

As could be seen in Figure 6.1, the second part of the questionnaire asked the teacher to check types of segments she thought elicited the most positive responses in the children. "Positive responses" were meant to indicate items of high attention value or active participation by the children during viewing. Figure 6.8 summarizes the results averaged across ratings of the 30 programs by all of the teachers participating in the diary study. As can be seen in this

FIGURE 6.1
SAMPLE PAGE--TEACHER DIARY   Date_____

Please give ratings by placing one check on each of the following scales:

1. THE PROGRAM FACILITATED LEARNING ACTIVITIES:

    very well ___:___:___:___:___:___:___ not at all

2. RELATIVE TO OTHER PROGRAMS IN THE SERIES, THIS PROGRAM WAS:

    better ___:___:___:___:___:___:___ poorer

3. RELATIVE TO THE CLASS LEVEL, THE PROGRAM CONTENT WAS:

    very appropriate ___:___:___:___:___:___:___ inappropriate

4. RELATIVE TO CLASS UNDERSTANDING, THE LANGUAGE LEVEL WAS:

    very appropriate ___:___:___:___:___:___:___ inappropriate

5. THE CHILDREN'S VERBAL PARTICIPATION WHEN PROMPTED BY THE PROGRAM WAS:

    high ___:___:___:___:___:___:___ low

6. THE PROGRAM HELD THE CHILDREN'S INTEREST:

    very well ___:___:___:___:___:___:___ not at all

Which segments elicited the most positive response from the children?
(Check one or more or identify a particular segment.)

___Animation   ___Puppets   ___Song
___Film   ___Marionettes   ___Guest appearances
___Dramatic   ___Concentration Board ___Other:_____

Please list further comments (a particular presentation technique or content
area which elicited a distinctive reaction, either positive or negative from
the children, or your own reactions as a teacher for this age level).

_____

_____

_____

_____

_____

_____

_____

_____

Did you put the date at the top of the page?

FIGURE 6.2

AVERAGE PROGRAM RATINGS BY GRADE LEVELS
APPROPRIATENESS OF CONTENT
SECOND YEAR EVALUATION

PROGRAM   RATING
NUMBER   SCALE

RELATIVE TO THE CLASS LEVEL, THE PROGRAM CONTENT WAS:
VERY APPROPRIATE   MIDPOINT   INAPPROPRIATE
1   2   3   4   5...7

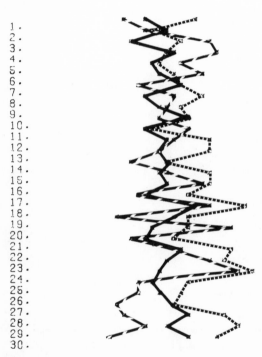

1.
2.
3.
4.
5.
6.
7.
8.
9.
10.
11.
12.
13.
14.
15.
16.
17.
18.
19.
20.
21.
22.
23.
24.
25.
26.
27.
28.
29.
30.

KEY

KINDERGARTEN
FIRST GRADE
SECOND GRADE

FIGURE 6.3

AVERAGE PROGRAM RATINGS BY GRADE LEVELS
APPROPRIATENESS OF LANGUAGE
SECOND YEAR EVALUATION

PROGRAM   RATING
NUMBER   SCALE

RELATIVE TO CLASS UNDERSTANDING THE LANGUAGE LEVEL WAS,
VERY APPROPRIATE   MIDPOINT   INAPPROPRIATE
1   2   3   4   5...7

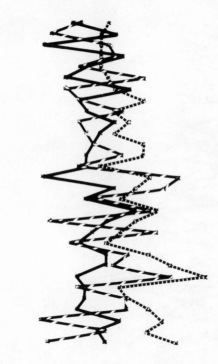

```
1.
2.
3.
4.
5.
6.
7.
8.
9.
10.
11.
12.
13.
14.
15.
16.
17.
18.
19.
20.
21.
22.
23.
24.
25.
26.
27.
28.
29.
30.
```

KEY

KINDERGARTEN   ······

FIRST GRADE   ——

SECOND GRADE   ⚹—

101

FIGURE 6.4

AVERAGE PROGRAM RATINGS BY GRADE LEVELS
CHILDREN'S INTEREST
SECOND YEAR EVALUATION

PROGRAM
NUMBER

RATING
SCALE

THE PROGRAM HELD THE CHILDREN'S INTEREST:
VERY WELL   MIDPOINT   NOT AT ALL
1   2   3   4   5...7

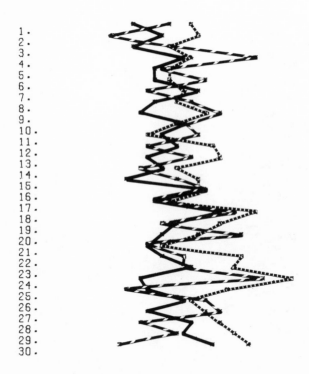

1.
2.
3.
4.
5.
6.
7.
8.
9.
10.
11.
12.
13.
14.
15.
16.
17.
18.
19.
20.
21.
22.
23.
24.
25.
26.
27.
28.
29.
30.

KEY
KINDERGARTEN ▪▪▪▪▪▪
FIRST GRADE ▬▬
SECOND GRADE ▬▬

FIGURE 6.5

AVERAGE PROGRAM RATINGS BY GRADE LEVELS
FACILITATION OF LEARNING ACTIVITIES
SECOND YEAR EVALUATION

PROGRAM   RATING
NUMBER   SCALE

THE PROGRAM FACILITATED LEARNING ACTIVITIES:
VERY WELL   MIDPOINT   NOT AT ALL
1   2   3   4   5...7

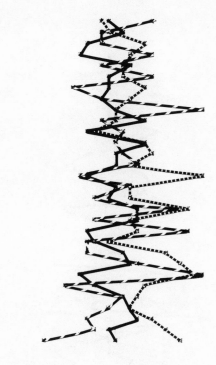

```
1.
2.
3.
4.
5.
6.
7.
8.
9.
10.
11.
12.
13.
14.
15.
16.
17.
18.
19.
20.
21.
22.
23.
24.
25.
26.
27.
28.
29.
30.
```

KEY
KINDERGARTEN   ------
FIRST GRADE   ——
SECOND GRADE   ——

103

FIGURE 6.6

AVERAGE PROGRAM RATINGS BY GRADE LEVELS
VERBAL PARTICIPATION WHEN PROMPTED BY THE PROGRAM
SECOND YEAR EVALUATION

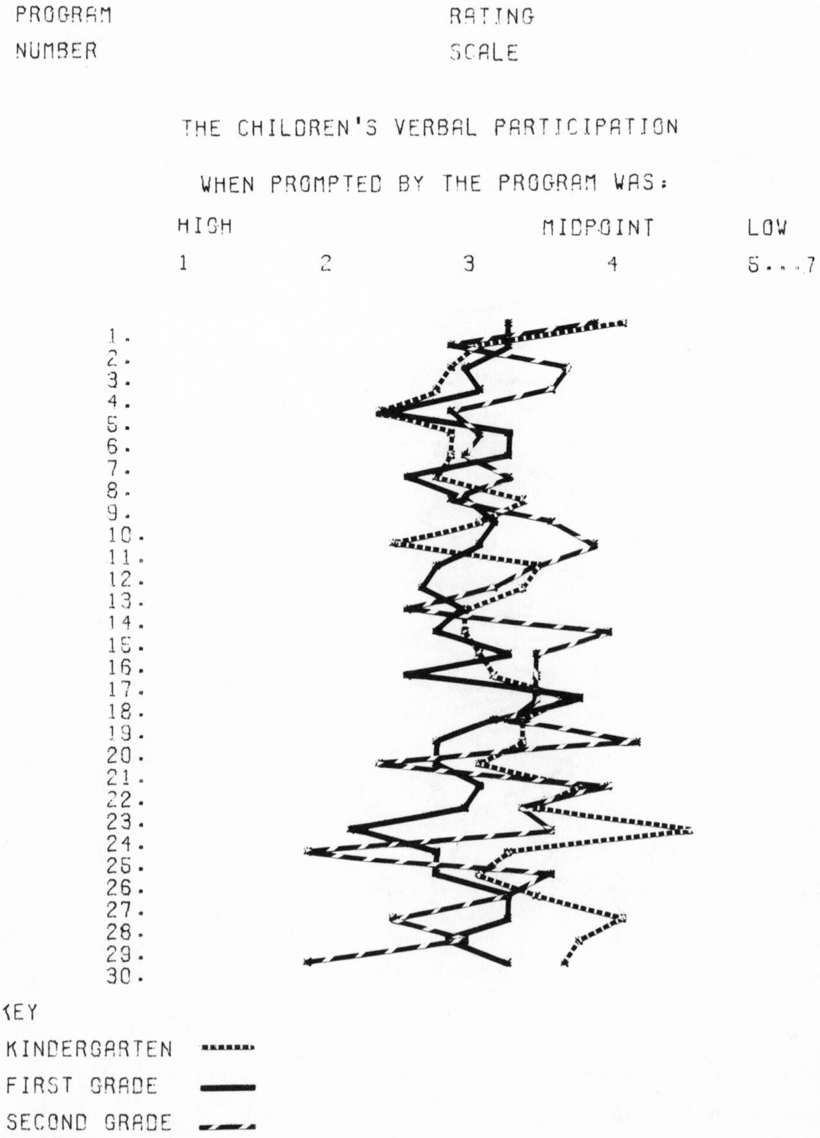

PROGRAM   RATING
NUMBER   SCALE

THE CHILDREN'S VERBAL PARTICIPATION

WHEN PROMPTED BY THE PROGRAM WAS:

HIGH   MIDPOINT   LOW

1   2   3   4   5...7

1.
2.
3.
4.
5.
6.
7.
8.
9.
10.
11.
12.
13.
14.
15.
16.
17.
18.
19.
20.
21.
22.
23.
24.
25.
26.
27.
28.
29.
30.

KEY

KINDERGARTEN   ▪▪▪▪▪▪▪

FIRST GRADE   ━━━━

SECOND GRADE   ━ ━ ━

104

FIGURE 6.7

AVERAGE PROGRAM RATINGS BY GRADE LEVELS
COMPARISON WITH OTHER PROGRAMS
SECOND YEAR EVALUATION

PROGRAM   RATING
NUMBER   SCALE

RELATIVE TO OTHER PROGRAMS IN THE SERIES, THE PROGRAM WAS:
BETTER   MIDPOINT   POORER
   1   2   3   4   5...7

1.
2.
3.
4.
5.
6.
7.
8.
9.
10.
11.
12.
13.
14.
15.
16.
17.
18.
19.
20.
21.
22.
23.
24.
25.
26.
27.
28.
29.
30.

KEY

KINDERGARTEN   ·······
FIRST GRADE   ━━━
SECOND GRADE   ━ ━

105

FIGURE 6.8

THIRTY PROGRAM RATING AVERAGES

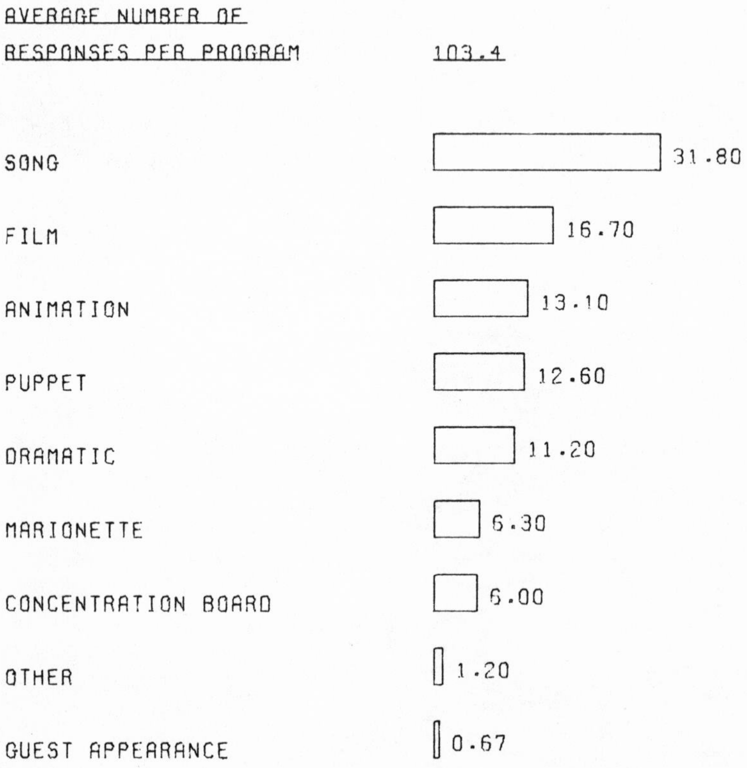

AVERAGE NUMBER OF
RESPONSES PER PROGRAM   103.4

SONG   31.80

FILM   16.70

ANIMATION   13.10

PUPPET   12.60

DRAMATIC   11.20

MARIONETTE   6.30

CONCENTRATION BOARD   6.00

OTHER   1.20

GUEST APPEARANCE   0.67

figure, songs were most frequently noted as eliciting positive responses, followed by films, animation, puppet sequences, and dramatic segments. Guest appearances, the concentration board, actor marionettes, and "other" segments received the lowest percentage of positive responses.

Teacher Comments

In the third section of the diary page, teachers were asked to record observations of their pupils as they viewed "Carrascolendas." Teachers were to note the pupils' attention level and participation during specific segments, the method of segment presentation, clarity of concepts, and coordination of content with classroom procedure. Comments illustrative of those that appeared most often in diaries including production techniques were:
too much stimulation in 30 minutes; have fewer programs with new
    material for each
the children benefited from the programs
need more child participation; children should be spoken to directly
    and asked to participate
math and science too advanced (kindergarten)
series invaluable; class response high
broadcast reruns in summer and at the end of the year when series
    ends
the show was excellent and the guide was useful
there was better structure for each show and I was glad to see a
    theme emerging for each show
background music often too loud
predominantly Anglo group did not benefit
like faster pace this year as compared to last year
history presentation was especially good
level of understanding too low for second grade
song repetition good
children are ready for more learning and less music and fun
more Spanish/English riddles
children and teacher aware of a unique and beautiful cultural heritage
Agapito (the lion) is great; he is the children's favorite
last year's puppets were better; puppets do not speak clearly enough
    in either language
the sounds were good; they did help the children understand Spanish
    words better
children enjoy animation, but words used to illustrate initial sounds
    should be easier and more familiar
children were attentive to films narrated in English, but not to those
    narrated in Spanish
film repetition in the same program is very boring

learning on the concentration board (similar to the board used on the
TV show by that name) is very effective

more techniques are needed for teaching math; the math segments
are not too short

the show needs more familiar children's songs

the songs were well done: the children learned them in English and
Spanish

cut out some English songs; use more in Spanish

THE THIRD YEAR: TEACHER RATINGS

Teacher Diaries used in the third year's evaluation were identical to the second year, except teachers were not asked to check which type of segments seemed to have the most positive responses. It was thought that this kind of information could be revealed in the comments for individual programs. A general-remarks page at the end of the diary was provided to permit comments about the series as a whole. Teachers who participated in the diary study in the third year of the project were selected by field consultants and were paid for completing the diary. Every six pages could be removed and placed in a return-mail envelope, which was bound in the diary. It was thus possible to summarize Teacher Diary evaluations on a biweekly basis during the third year and to present this information to the program production staff.

Thirty-two teachers completed the diaries representing the following test sites: Albuquerque, Edinburg, Lansing, Los Angeles, San Antonio, Tracy, and Tucson. These represented feedback from 10 kindergarten, 12 first-grade, and 10 second-grade teachers. About 75 percent of the teachers reported that their classes were largely comprised of Mexican-American children, with a large spread of capabilities in English and Spanish-language fluency reported for the children. About 25 percent of the teachers spoke no Spanish; half of them spoke it fluently, and the remainder had some degree of fluency. Over half of the teachers also had an aide who spoke Spanish fluently. Only 9 of the 32 teachers had classes that viewed the program in color.

Figures 6.9 to 6.14 summarize the average ratings of the 30 programs provided by kindergarten, first-, and second-grade teachers. Each of these figures represents summary results for a particular rating scale, and left-to-right deviations of the lines in the figures represent distinctions between positive (left, or small numbers) and negative (right, or large numbers) ratings. Generally, as can be seen in all of the figures, the programs were rated in the positive half of the scale.

Beyond the general positive level of the ratings, a further generalization was that second-grade ratings tended to be the highest for

FIGURE 6.9

AVERAGE PROGRAM RATINGS BY GRADE LEVELS
APPROPRIATENESS OF CONTENT

PROGRAM   RATING
NUMBER   SCALE

RELATIVE TO THE CLASS LEVEL, THE PROGRAM CONTENT WAS:
VERY APPROPRIATE   MIDPOINT   INAPPROPRIATE
1   2   3   4   5...7

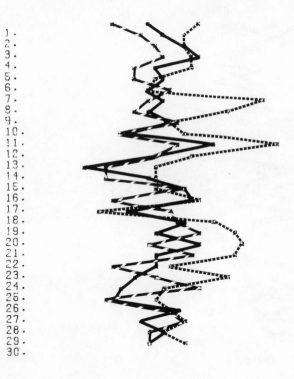

KEY

KINDERGARTEN ▪▪▪▪▪

FIRST GRADE ▬▬

SECOND GRADE ▭▭

FIGURE 6.10

AVERAGE PROGRAM RATINGS BY GRADE LEVELS
APPROPRIATENESS OF LANGUAGE

PROGRAM   RATING
NUMBER   SCALE

RELATIVE TO CLASS UNDERSTANDING THE LANGUAGE LEVEL WAS:
VERY APPROPRIATE   MIDPOINT   INAPPROPRIATE
1   2   3   4   5...7

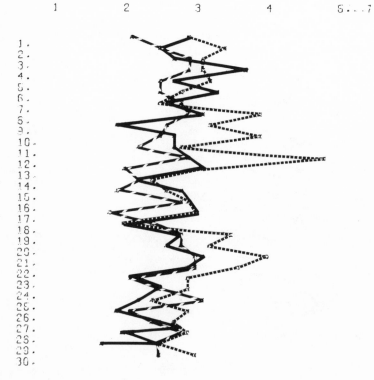

KEY

KINDERGARTEN ~~~~~

FIRST GRADE ━━━

SECOND GRADE ━ ━

110

FIGURE 6.11

AVERAGE PROGRAM RATINGS BY GRADE LEVELS
CHILDREN'S INTEREST

PROGRAM   RATING
NUMBER   SCALE

THE PROGRAM HELD THE CHILDREN'S INTEREST.
VERY WELL   MIDPOINT   NOT AT ALL
  1   2   3   4   5...7

KEY

KINDERGARTEN ......

FIRST GRADE ▬▬

SECOND GRADE ▬·

111

FIGURE 6.12

AVERAGE PROGRAM RATINGS BY GRADE LEVELS
FACILITATION OF LEARNING ACTIVITIES

PROGRAM   RATING
NUMBER   SCALE

THE PROGRAM FACILITATED LEARNING ACTIVITIES:
VERY WELL   MIDPOINT   NOT AT ALL
1   2   3   4   5...7

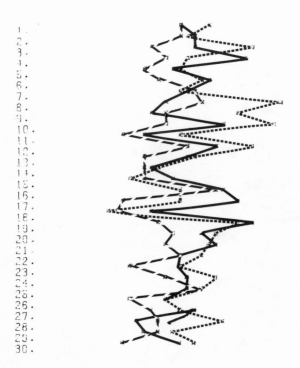

KEY
KINDERGARTEN ·····
FIRST GRADE ——
SECOND GRADE — —

112

FIGURE 6.13

AVERAGE PROGRAM RATINGS BY GRADE LEVELS
VERBAL PARTICIPATION WHEN PROMPTED BY THE PROGRAM

PROGRAM   RATING
NUMBER   SCALE

THE CHILDREN'S VERBAL PARTICIPATION

WHEN PROMPTED BY THE PROGRAM WAS:

HIGH   MIDPOINT   LOW
1   2   3   4   5...7

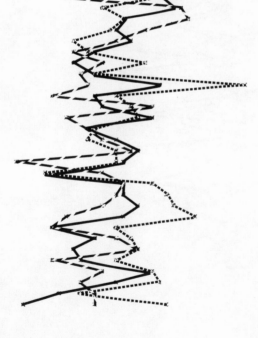

KEY
KINDERGARTEN ------
FIRST GRADE   ———
SECOND GRADE .—.

113

FIGURE 6.14

AVERAGE PROGRAM RATINGS BY GRADE LEVELS
COMPARISON WITH OTHER PROGRAMS

PROGRAM
NUMBER

RATING
SCALE

RELATIVE TO OTHER PROGRAMS IN THE SERIES, THE PROGRAM W
BETTER   MIDPOINT   POORER
    1   2   3   4   5...7

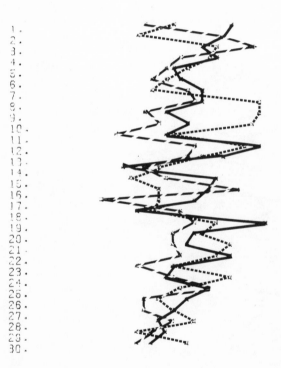

KEY

KINDERGARTEN ------
FIRST GRADE ———
SECOND GRADE --—

114

the 30 programs on all of the scales, with kindergarten usually rated somewhat lower, and first grade in the middle. According to teachers' ratings there are some programs that are more effective for one grade level than another. The overall rating profile suggests that the series tends to be most appropriate for second graders. However, even when kindergarten ratings are lower, there are only a few programs where this was in the negative half of the scale.

We noted also that, although ratings deviated on a program-to-program basis, there was no overall trend across the 30 programs, such as ratings becoming generally more positive or more negative. This suggests that the series was consistent in rated qualities across all 30 programs. A final point is that ratings on the different scales were often related. That is, as a teacher tended to rate, say, "program content" in terms of its level, such ratings were related to ratings of "understanding," or of the children's "interest," and the like. In short, the rating scales are relatively interrelated, and a future question might be whether six separate ones are needed.

Average Ratings for Different Sites

The same evaluation data were also analyzed in terms of average rating at each site, and these results are summarized in Figures 6.15 to 6.21. In each of these figures, the six rating scales are given for a test site and the average ratings on each of those scales across the 30 programs by the teacher evaluators of that site are plotted. For reference purposes, the average of all sites is plotted on each of these figures, so it is possible to see whether the particular ratings on the scales were above or below the overall average for each site.

One finding that stands out in the comparison of these figures is that the Edinburg, San Antonio, and Los Angeles teachers gave much higher average ratings to the programs than did teachers at any of the other sites. It may be recalled that Edinburg is in a predominantly Mexican-American part of Texas. The lowest average ratings came from the Tucson group in evaluation of "content"; however, this rating was only slightly below the midpoint on the scale. Albuquerque, Lansing, and Tracy ratings were slightly lower than the combined site ratings, but still well above the midpoint.

Teacher Comments

As in the second year's evaluation, comments were collated and placed into categories according to the frequency of occurrence. A frequent comment on the third year's evaluation was that songs and animation were the most popular means of instruction for the children. Films were enjoyed, although the degree of attention varied

FIGURE 6.15

ALBUQUERQUE RATINGS OF CARRASCOLENDAS
(Average of 30 Programs)

The program facilitated learning
activities:
very well..............not at all

Relative to other programs in the
series, this program was:
better.................poorer

Relative to the class level, the
program content was:
very appropriate....inappropriate

Relative to class understanding,
the language level was:
very appropriate....inappropriate

The children's verbal participation
when prompted by the program was:
high...................low

The program held the children's
interest:
very well..............not at all

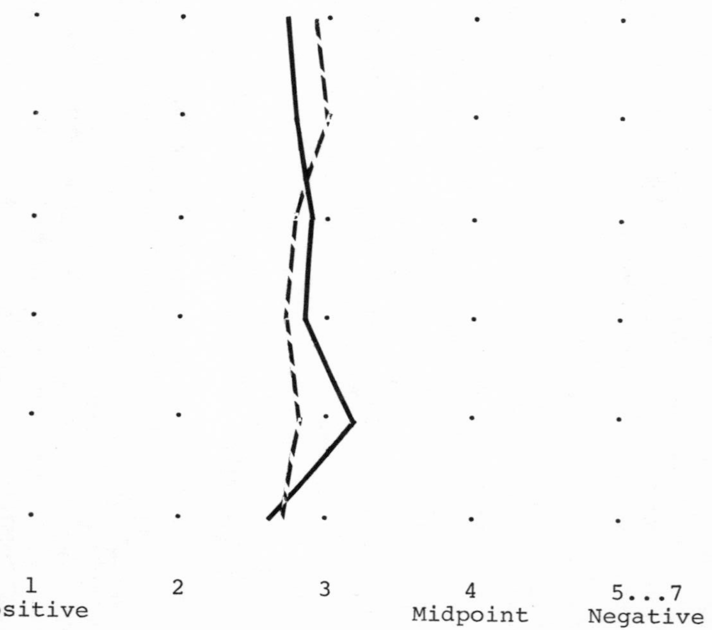

1	2	3	4	5...7
Positive			Midpoint	Negative

Site Ratings
Combined Sites Ratings

FIGURE 6.16

EDINBURG RATINGS OF <u>CARRASCOLENDAS</u>
(Average of 30 Programs)

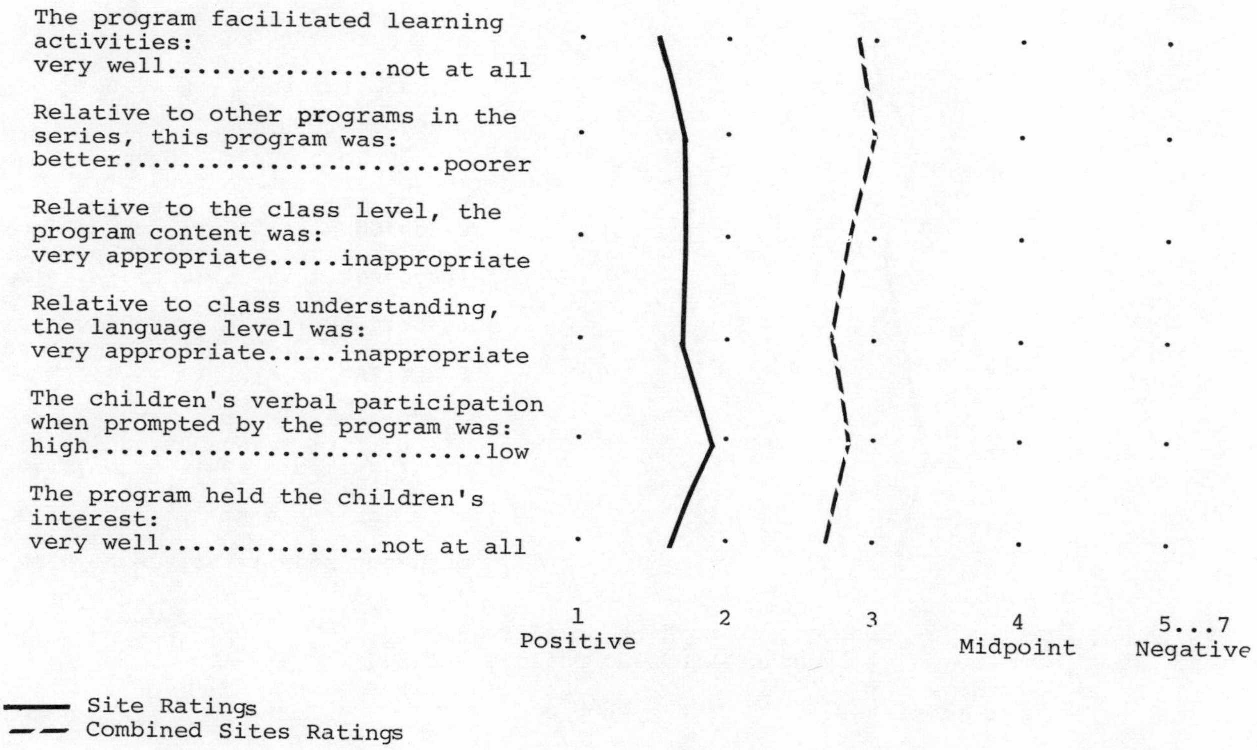

The program facilitated learning
activities:
very well............not at all

Relative to other programs in the
series, this program was:
better.................poorer

Relative to the class level, the
program content was:
very appropriate.....inappropriate

Relative to class understanding,
the language level was:
very appropriate.....inappropriate

The children's verbal participation
when prompted by the program was:
high..................low

The program held the children's
interest:
very well............not at all

1	2	3	4	5...7
Positive			Midpoint	Negative

▬▬ Site Ratings
▬ ▬ Combined Sites Ratings

117

FIGURE 6.17

LANSING RATINGS OF CARRASCOLENDAS
(Average of 30 Programs)

The program facilitated learning
activities:
very well...............not at all

Relative to other programs in the
series, this program was:
better................poorer

Relative to the class level, the
program content was:
very appropriate.....inappropriate

Relative to class understanding,
the language level was:
very appropriate.....inappropriate

The children's verbal participation
when prompted by the program was:
high....................low

The program held the children's
interest:
very well...............not at all

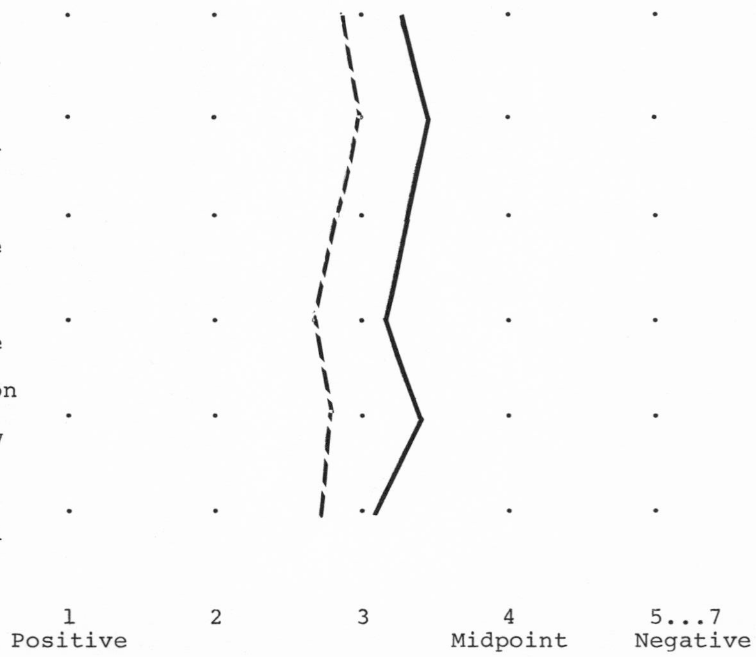

1	2	3	4	5...7
Positive			Midpoint	Negative

FIGURE 6.18

SAN ANTONIO RATINGS OF CARRASCOLENDAS
(Average of 30 Programs)

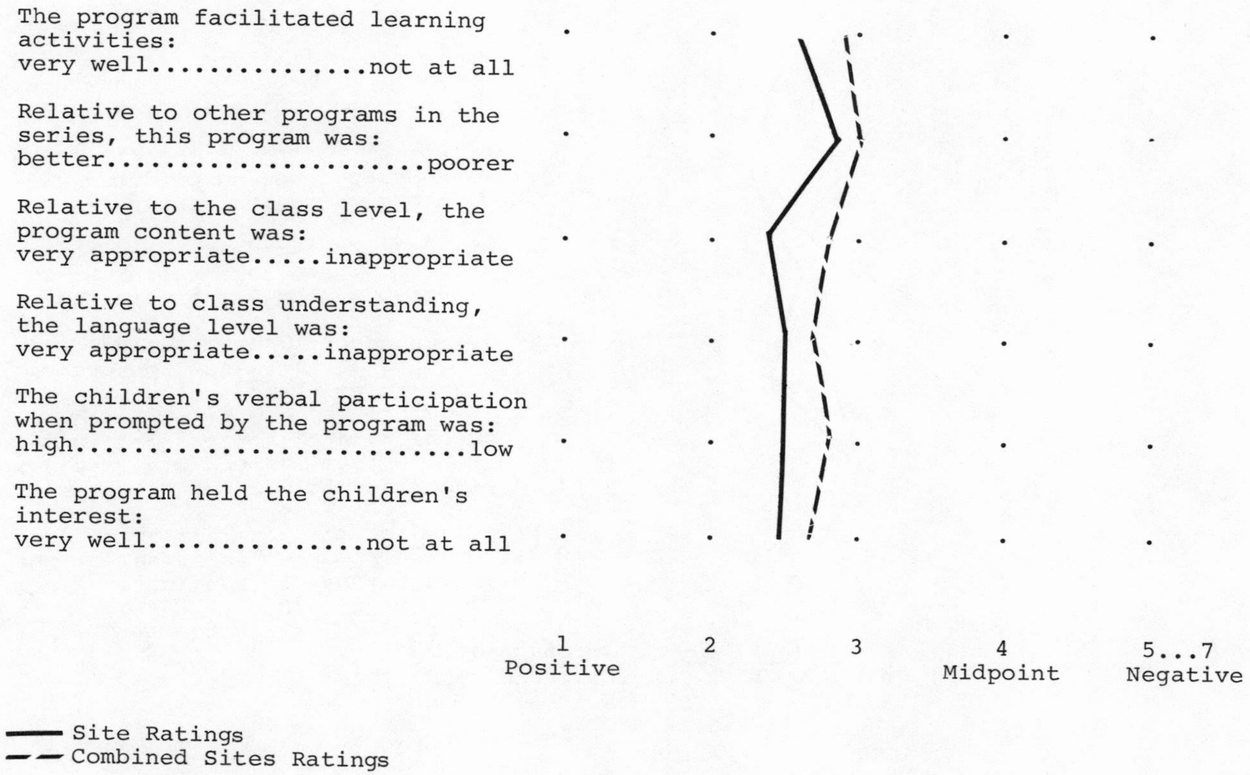

The program facilitated learning
activities:
very well............not at all

Relative to other programs in the
series, this program was:
better.................poorer

Relative to the class level, the
program content was.....inappropriate
very appropriate....inappropriate

Relative to class understanding,
the language level was:
very appropriate.....inappropriate

The children's verbal participation
when prompted by the program was:
high.................low

The program held the children's
interest:
very well............not at all

1	2	3	4	5...7
Positive			Midpoint	Negative

━━ Site Ratings
╌╌ Combined Sites Ratings

119

FIGURE 6.19

LOS ANGELES RATINGS OF CARRASCOLENDAS
(Average of 30 Programs)

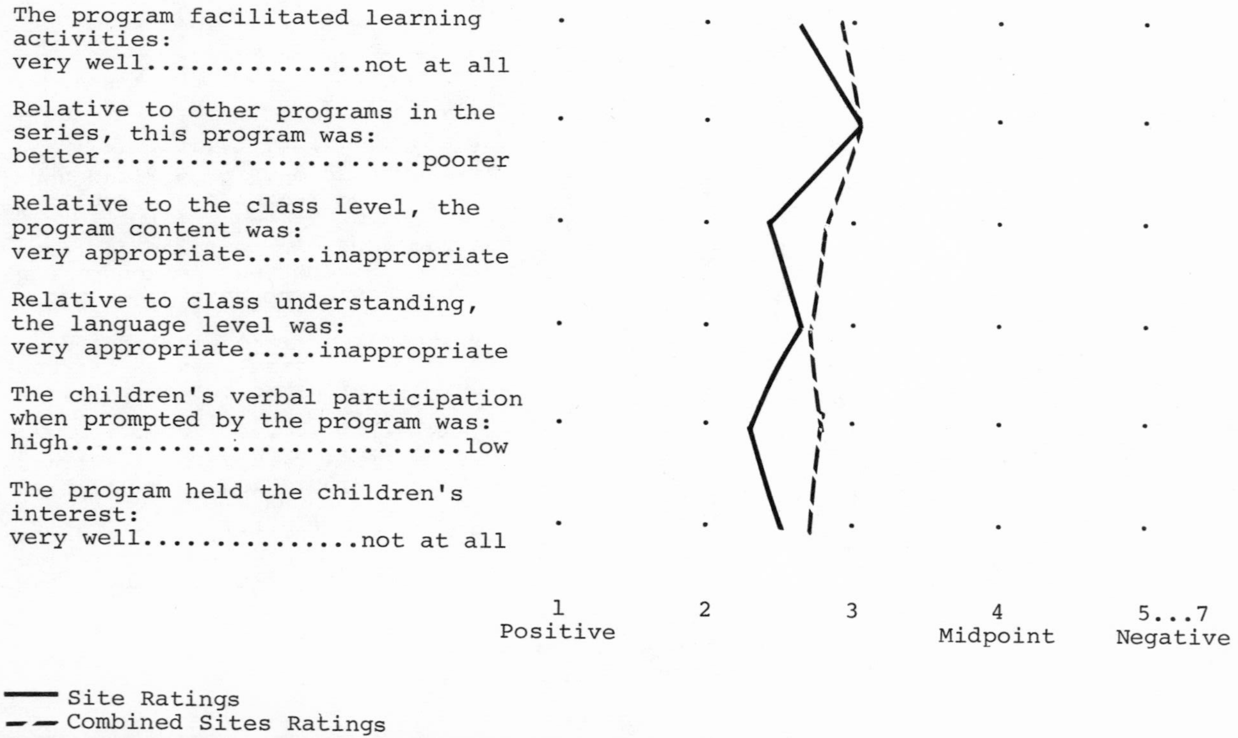

The program facilitated learning
activities:
very well.............not at all

Relative to other programs in the
series, this program was:
better...............poorer

Relative to the class level, the
program content was:
very appropriate.....inappropriate

Relative to class understanding,
the language level was:
very appropriate.....inappropriate

The children's verbal participation
when prompted by the program was:
high.................low

The program held the children's
interest:
very well.............not at all

| 1 | 2 | 3 | 4 | 5...7 |
| Positive | | | Midpoint | Negative |

—— Site Ratings
– – Combined Sites Ratings

120

FIGURE 6.20

TRACY RATINGS OF <u>CARRASCOLENDAS</u>
(Average of 30 Programs)

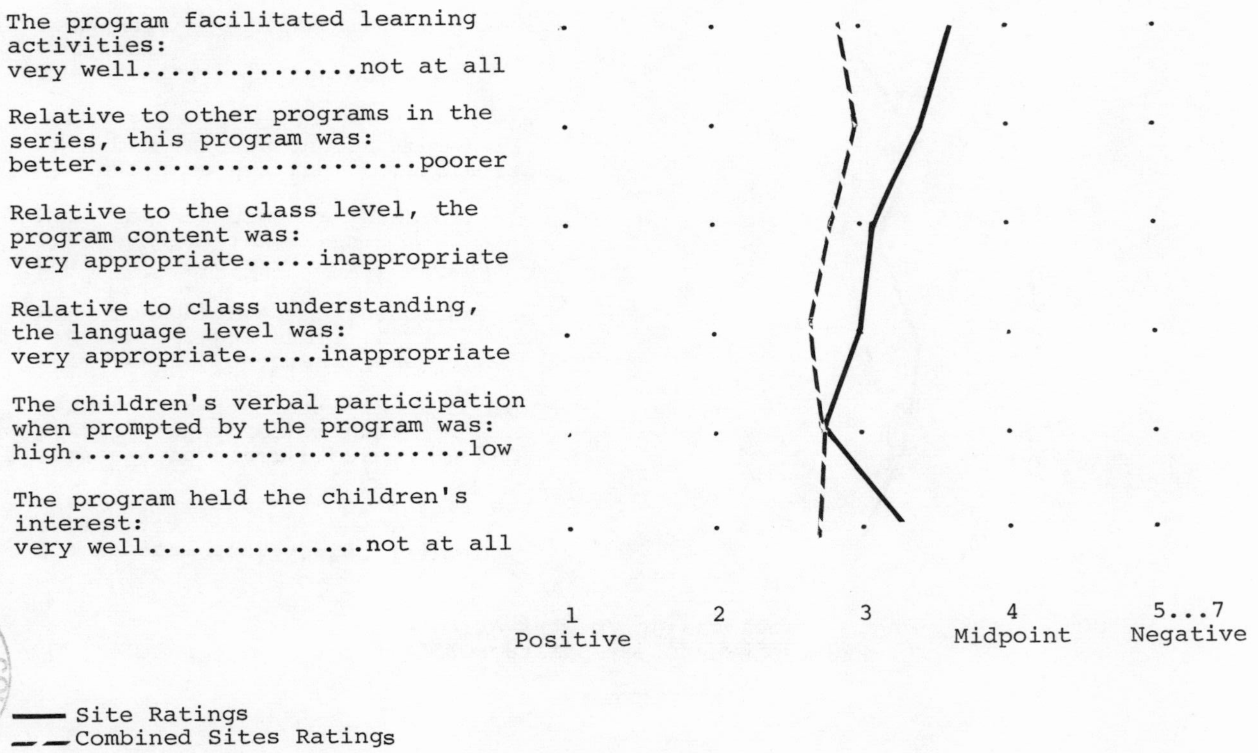

The program facilitated learning
activities:
very well............not at all

Relative to other programs in the
series, this program was:
better..................poorer

Relative to the class level, the
program content was:
very appropriate....inappropriate

Relative to class understanding,
the language level was:
very appropriate....inappropriate

The children's verbal participation
when prompted by the program was:
high....................low

The program held the children's
interest:
very well............not at all

1   2   3   4   5...7
Positive   Midpoint   Negative

——— Site Ratings
— — Combined Sites Ratings

121

FIGURE 6.21

TUCSON RATINGS OF CARRASCOLENDAS
(Average of 30 Programs)

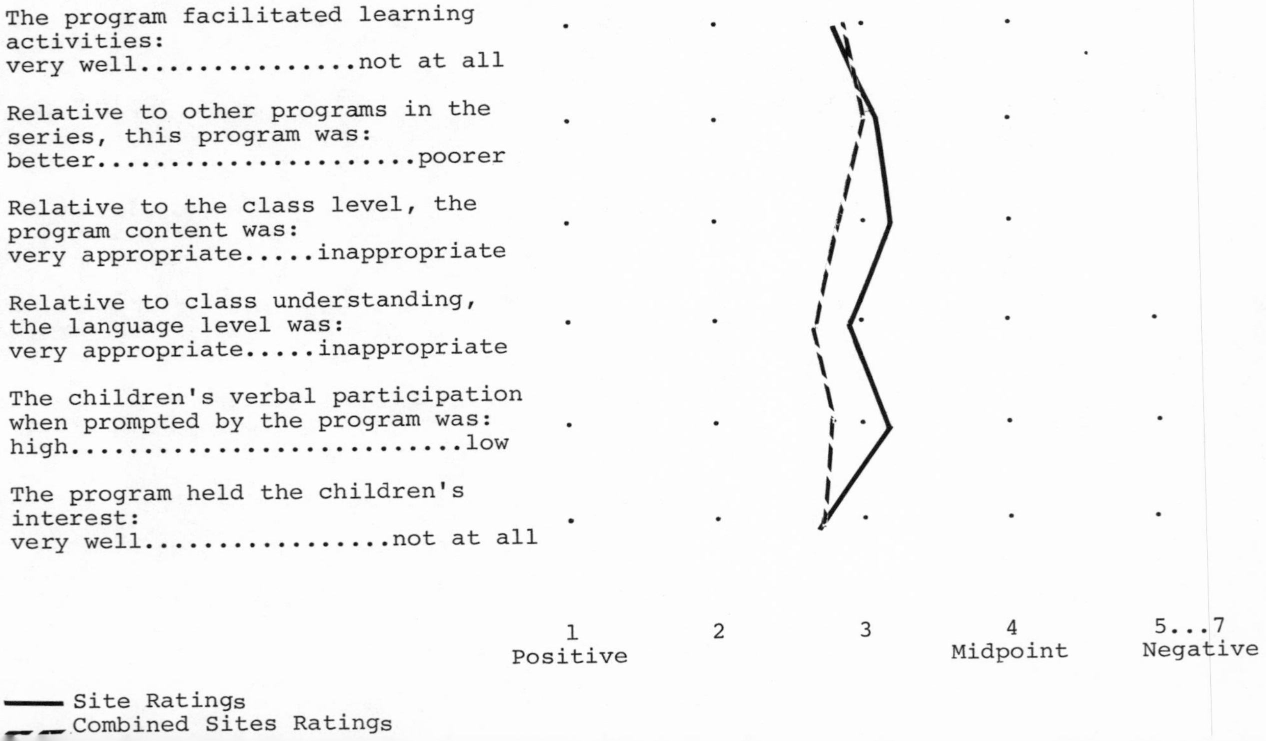

The program facilitated learning
activities:
very well............not at all

Relative to other programs in the
series, this program was:
better.................poorer

Relative to the class level, the
program content was:
very appropriate....inappropriate

Relative to class understanding,
the language level was:
very appropriate....inappropriate

The children's verbal participation
when prompted by the program was:
high.................low

The program held the children's
interest:
very well............not at all

| 1 | 2 | 3 | 4 | 5...7 |
| Positive | | | Midpoint | Negative |

Site Ratings
Combined Sites Ratings

122

for a particular film. The animation segments elicited most of the audience participation for the entire series; there was much participation in songs once the lyrics were learned. The puppets were attractive to children, but their dialogues were often unclear, thereby detracting from the content of the segment. Agapito continued to be the favorite character; however, the amusing segments, regardless of characters, generally had high appeal for the children.

Collated remarks from the general-remarks page are as follows (no kindergarten teachers commented):

1. First grade
wonderful educational and rewarding program
children learn by participation
children are more open with teacher and peers
children are encouraged to have more pride in their native tongue and culture

2. Second grade
activities on show well planned, and therefore interesting and easy to understand
impressive show
children enjoy the characters, especially Agapito
children's interest would be higher if puppets spoke more clearly
interested in seeing the series again

SUMMARY

In the third year, responses to the Teacher Diary indicated very favorable reactions to "Carrascolendas" by teachers of kindergarten, first, and second grades. Program 8 received high ratings from the combined sites as did Programs 12 and 17. When considered according to grade levels, the lowest (positive) average ratings elicited were from kindergarten teachers, followed by first- and second-grade teachers respectively. Site responses indicated most positive ratings of the series from Edinburg, with Lansing and Tracy rating the series lowest. However, all ratings ranked toward the higher end of the scales (lower than 4). Overall responses were very positive, with teachers indicating that songs, animation, and films were the segments most appealing to children.

7

PROMOTING
CLASSROOM ACTIVITIES

The need was felt for an adjunct to the television series that would enhance the educational experience of the child and organize this experience for the teacher. To meet this need, a Teacher Guide was developed to accompany "Carrascolendas." The Guide was deemed necessary to encourage teachers to provide children with "doing" as well as "viewing" experiences. Its goal was to affect behavior. Children would be able to participate in classroom activities that were elaborations of the ideas presented in each program. The television presentations could not always include all facets of each behavioral objective and sometimes only an intriguing taste of a concept was presented. Therefore the Guide was able to offer an expansion of concept and ideas. This made it possible for the teacher to encourage classroom activities, which would have been difficult to illustrate in the series or were not shown with enough emphasis or details.

For the monolingual English-speaking teachers, the Guide provided insight into the Mexican-American culture. It helped the teachers see the rationale behind the behavioral objectives. In this way it was hoped that "Carrascolendas"-inspired activities would become closely tied and pertinent to the regular curriculum of the classroom.

Having strong family ties both in the United States and in Mexico, the curriculum coordinator was completely bilingual and creatively adept in her use of both Spanish and English. She brought to her job more than 20 years of experience in teaching both languages to Spanish speakers and English speakers.* She speculated that the Guide played a significant role in the teacher's activities before and after watching "Carrascolendas." Without the Guide, teachers probably would not have developed related activities, except perhaps a minimal amount of discussion or art work. Thus the purpose of the Teacher Guide

---

*The curriculum coordinator was Carol Perkins of Austin, Texas.

was to provide a resource manual from which teachers could glean
ideas and concrete projects to carry out with the children.

DESIGN AND REVISIONS

The curriculum coordinator and her staff of consultants had no
prototype on which to base the content or format of the Teacher Guide.
Initially, objectives and Guide construction evolved intuitively from
their individual teaching experiences. The first Teacher Guide prepared for "Carrascolendas" was a looseleaf notebook containing activities and pictures illustrating different sounds and animals. The pictures could be used by teachers in developing such visual aids as puppets and puzzles; they could be cut out and pasted on cardboard for
repeated use, or mounted on felt for feltboards. Figure 7.1 gives
examples of a lesson plan page, a vocabulary card page, and a clear,
step-by-step description of a game from the first year's Guide. The
lesson plan page describes three different kinds of activities. The
first relates to the concept of set and the ability to generalize similarities and differences. The teacher can provide concrete sets of objects
to illustrate the point. The next activity uses pictures to encourage
practice of the syntactical use of does in English. The last activity
encourages cooperation in group functions, an important aspect of
socialization.

In the second year, informal feedback to the curriculum coordinator and comments in the Teacher Diary section of the first
year's evaluation prompted changes in the next edition of the Guide.
In order to prepare better warm-up and follow-up activities for viewer
children, teachers asked for more detailed descriptions of the segments
to be shown in each program. They asked for the words to all songs,
suggesting that the music be included for use with a piano. Teachers
suggested that pictures be printed on only one side of the page, so
that they could be cut out. A table of contents and clearer organization of the Guide were requested. The revised format clearly coordinated the concepts, behavioral objectives, content, and related
aids and activities for each program. The looseleaf notebook was
replaced by a bound volume plus a packet of sheets to be used as visual
aids, the Visuals Kit. This new Guide was organized according to
activities for specific skill areas. The first half of the Guide was a
compilation of descriptions of each program, segment by segment.
Words to all the songs and poems were included the first time they
were presented. When they were repeated during subsequent programs, only the titles were given. The behavioral objectives and
hints to the teacher for classroom elaboration were stated after
pertinent segments. The second half of the Guide listed and described
lesson plans, games, recipes, and other activities related to the seven
content areas: English language skills, Spanish language skills, his-
tory/culture, math skills, reading skills, science, and self-concept.

FIGURE 7.1

TEACHER GUIDE EXAMPLES:

A-8 Sorting of Sets

Lesson Plan Page

Use Rhyming Word cards (I 14-15) for this activity. Ask a child to find:

1. All the animals; all the animals with 4 legs, all the animals with 2 legs; the animals with no legs.

2. All the parts of the body

3. Things to eat, food that comes from plants, food that comes from animals.

4. Things that are made in factories, things Mother could make, things children could make.

5. Things that have metal in them.

6. All the triangles, all the big circles, all the little squares

The teacher collects:

a set of big things

a set of little things.

a set of things to cut with (knife, paper cutter, scissors, nail clippers, etc.)

a set of things made of glass

The child labels the sets.

In both of the above activities, the teacher should reward those who succeed with points for their groups.

A-9 English Language Skills: He doesn't _____ .

Looking at either fish or baby picture (I-12), the child can make a point for his side each time he makes a sentence starting with *He doesn't* _____ . He says: "Here's a fish. He doesn't climb; he doesn't sit; he doesn't walk; he doesn't cook . . ." (He does the same thing with picture of the baby.)

A-10 Division of Labor—Cooperation

"We can get a lot done if we divide up the work" is the idea we want to put across in this activity.

Using a-e-i-o-u groups, make a schedule for cleaning up the room every Friday.

The children in each group decide how they will divide up the work. (Other activities that go along with this idea: making tacos, giving a party, making a mural.)

FIGURE 7.1 (Continued)

Vocabulary Card Page

I-27

piña

cigüeña

niña

cinco

cepillo

cebra

borrego

barril

burro

127

FIGURE 7.1 (Continued)

Game Description

Mata Rile Rile Ro comes from the French game: Un beau bateau. The Spanish translate those sounds to Amó ató.

The players are divided into two groups facing each other. The first row advances and bows and sings a question, then returns to its place.

The second row does the same thing as they answer. The line: "Ese oficio sí le gusta" is the cue for players to join hands and walk around in a circle. This continues until the song ends.

a AMÓ ATÓ
   MATA RILE RILE RO

b ¿QUÉ QUIERE USTED?
   MATA RILE RILE RO

a LE PONDREMOS PLANCHADORA
   MATA RILE RILE RO

a YO QUIERO UN PAJE
   MATA RILE RILE RO

b ESE OFICIO NO LE GUSTA
   MATA RILE RILE RO

b ESCOJA USTED
   MATA RILE RILE RO

a LE PONDREMOS COSTURERA
   MATA RILE RILE RO

a YO ESCOJO A ROSA*
   MATA RILE RILE RO

b ESE OFICIO NO LE GUSTA
   MATA RILE RILE RO

b ¿QUÉ OFICIO LE PONDREMOS?
   MATA RILE RILE RO

a LE PONDREMOS REINA HERMOSA
   MATA RILE RILE RO

a LE PONDREMOS COCINERA
   MATA RILE RILE RO

*Use names of members of the class.

b ESE OFICIO NO LE GUSTA
   MATA RILE RILE RO

FIGURE 7.1 (Continued)

b ESE OFICIO SÍ LE GUSTA
   MATA RILE RILE RO

a AQUÍ LE ENTREGO A MI HIJA
   MATA RILE RILE RO

b SI NO LE HACE LOS MANDADOS
   LE DARÁ SU COSCORRÓN

a AMÓ ATÓ
   MATA RILE RILE RO

b ¿QUÉ QUIERE USTED?
   MATA RILE RILE RO

a CELEBREMOS TODOS JUNTOS
   MATA RILE RILE RO

a CELEBREMOS TODOS JUNTOS
   MATA RILE RILE RO

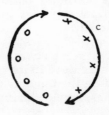

G-3

San Serafín del Monte

SAN SERAFÍN DEL MONTE
SAN SERAFÍN CORDERO
YO COMO BUEN CRISTIANO
ME *HINCARÉ*

SAN SERAFÍN DEL MONTE
SAN SERAFÍN CORDERO
YO COMO BUEN CRISTIANO
ME *SENTARÉ*

SAN SERAFÍN DEL MONTE
SAN SERAFÍN CORDERO
YO COMO BUEN CRISTIANO
ME ACOSTARÉ

SAN SERAFÍN DEL MONTE
SAN SERAFÍN CORDERO
YO COMO BUEN CRISTIANO
ME *ARRASTRARÉ*

SAN SERAFÍN DEL MONTE
SAN SERAFÍN CORDERO
YO COMO BUEN CRISTIANO
ME *PARARÉ*

SAN SERAFÍN DEL MONTE
SAN SERAFÍN CORDERO
YO COMO BUEN CRISTIANO
ME *REIRÉ*

The players stand in a semicircle while a leader acts out what he wants them to do. Then the children imitate him. (This song teaches children many kinds of verbs in Spanish.)

129

The Guide's last 15 pages were devoted to reference lists of music, games, visuals, and activities, as well as the 1972 spring program schedule. For the second year only, tapes of the songs in the Guide were made available to teachers. However, the time and expense required to produce these tapes made their continued production, as a supplementary aid to the project, unsuitable.

The third year's Guide was very similar to the second. It retained the Visuals Kit and the simple, appealing black and white illustrations from the preceding year. The organization was improved by grouping all relevant activities under the appropriate content heading in the "List of Activities." Within each program description, page numbers were provided indicating where songs and activities could be found in the Guide. When songs or rhymes were repeated in the program, page numbers were listed next to the title to facilitate teacher reference. Because the Guide is often used by monolingual English-speaking educators, ample clarification of the programs' Spanish content was provided.

OVERALL FORMAT

The title page of the Guide describes its theme of providing activities for children individually, in small groups, and in large groups. Teachers were encouraged to try all of these types and not rely solely on activities that involved the whole class of some 30 children at the same time.

Many of the activities in the Guide were created and tailored originally for the Guide and for "Carrascolendas." Carrying out the behavioral objectives was a central focus for selecting activities, songs, games, and the like. For example, in the following song the children can practice the vowel sound of bit, pick, hit, rhythm, and twist, as it does not occur in Spanish. Many children use instead the vowel sound of beat when pronouncing bit.

A Bit of A Beat

Bit, beat, bit, beat, bit, beat, bit, beat.
Tap your feet, pull a bit, tap your feet,
    pull a bit,
Bit, beat, bit, beat, bit, beat, bit, beat,
Pick the pace, hit the beat, pick the pace,
    hit the beat,
Bit, beat, bit, beat, bit, beat, bit, beat.

Shuffle, Shuffle, bit by bit,
To the rhythm of the beat,
Stomp and shake, and dance a bit,

Twist and turn and tap your feet.
Pick the pace and pull a bit,
Shuffle, shuffle to the beat,
To the rhythm, bit by bit,
Shake and dance and hit the beat.

Another song emphasizes irregular plurals in English.

More Than One

Hey, come along and have some fun
With words that mean "more than one."
If I say tooth, you say teeth,
If I say foot, you say feet.

Hey, come along, and have some fun
With words that mean "more than one."
If I say mouse, you don't say meese.

Hey, come along and have some fun
With words that mean "more than one."
If I say mouse, you say mice,
If I say man, you say men.

While fulfilling the essential behavioral objective criterion, each activity was chosen with a view to its intrinsic interest, stimulation, humor, and fun. The writing of poems and sketches, and the composition of music and lyrics for songs, were often the result of a collaboration of two or more people's ideas about how to present a particular objective. In the area of history/culture the attempt was made to capture special family relationships. An example of this is the particular warmth that exists between many a Mexican-American child and his/her grandmother.

Figure 7.2 is a reproduction of the Teacher Guide's treatment of Program 19 described in Chapter 2. The teacher can read the list of segments before viewing the program and note suggestions for related activities. For example, a description of the film includes suggestions for elaboration and a list of Spanish terms; both could be incorporated into a pre- or postviewing activity. A previewing activity has the advantage of stimulating the child's interest and curiosity while giving him a familiar "handle" for the information he will see later in the program.

The curriculum coordinator's major philosophy of learning in general, and language learning in particular, is that it be active, energetic, vigorous, and reinforcing in a continuous, positive way. Children cannot be passive recipients of knowledge and skills; they must be given much varied opportunity for practicing new skills.

131

FIGURE 7.2

PROGRAM 19

SPANISH LANGUAGE SKILLS

El cuento de nunca acabar.

MATH - Zero - The Empty Set

Agapito and Sr. Villarreal start out with 4 balloons and end up with NONE.

cuatro globos	- 4 balloons
menos uno	- minus one
cero	- zero

INITIAL SOUNDS GÜ/gw/

The combination gü before e or i is presented medially with its corresponding sounds, as it seldom occurs initially.

Note that the gue and gui syllables in the preceding program and the güe and güi syllables in this program have different sounds.

cigüeña - stork	paragüitas - little umbrella

SONG ♪ 141

The World Is Round (repeat)

FILM - The Truck ✸ 100

This film takes us out on the highway to see something of what is involved in a truck driver's profession. This is a good time to discuss natural versus man-made environment as the film shows us such items as highways, bridges, and overpasses which children should recognize and be able to discuss regarding their functions.

SPANISH TERMS:

el camión	- truck
combustible diesel	- diesel fuel
la carretera	- highway
el puente	- bridge
el puente elevado	- overpass

FIGURE 7.2 (Continued)

EL ANILLO

INITIAL SOUNDS GÜ/gw/

Guillermina es güera.*
Guillermina is a blonde.

La cigüeña es alta.
The stork is tall.

*Here gü may be heard initially.

PIN MARÍN

SONG ♫ 138

Side by Side (repeat)

SCIENCE - The Falling Ball ✿ 120

Agapito and Tina get their gravity lesson in Spanish
from Mr. Villarreal.

SPANISH TERMS:

fuerza de gravedad	- force of gravity
elástico	- elastic
esta pelota	- this ball
la tierra	- the earth
atrae el libro	- attracts the book

INITIAL SOUNDS G/g/ (repeat) ✿ 117, 118 Dice Game

LA VELA

SCIENCE - Gravity Has Pull ✿ 120

Willy playing with a ball learns about gravity.

SONG ♫ 134

Naricita, Naricita (repeat)

MATH - Subtraction

We start out with 4 lighted windows and we end up with
none.

cuatro ventanas alumbradas - four lighted windows
menos una - minus one

FIGURE 7.2 (Continued)

LA NAVAJA (repeat)

INITIAL SOUNDS GU/g/ (repeat)

ENGLISH LANGUAGE SKILLS - On and In ✿ 87

This segment shows children on a bus, on a train, on the floor, on a chair, and in a car.

Uses of "on" in English are difficult for Spanish speakers who generalize, "If I can say 'on a bus,' 'on a bicycle,' 'on a train,' I can say 'on a car.'" This last expression would have a very different meaning from "in the car" which is what a native speaker of English would say.

SONG ♫ 129

La Vieja Inés (repeat)

MATH - La Resta - Subtraction

Agapito pops two of five balloons and has three left.

Cinco globos menos dos?
Five balloons less two?

EL PLÁTANO

MEDIAL SOUNDS - Gü/gw/ (repeat)

SONG ♫ 139

B and V (repeat)

SPANISH LANGUAGE SKILLS - Riddles

¿Qué le dijo el zapato al amo?

Activities suggested in the Guide are means for supplying greater involvement of teachers and students viewing "Carrascolendas."

EVALUATIONS

As a part of the overall evaluation, teachers were asked questions regarding their use of the Teacher Guide. An evaluation form was structured during the second year to give information on class composition, the teacher's fluency in Spanish, the frequency of viewing the series, and usage of the Teacher Guide. A sample copy of the questionnaire is found in Appendix D. Five statements regarding the content and usefulness of the Teacher Guide in various areas were rated on a seven-point scale. Blanks were available for teacher comment about changes she/he might be interested in making.

The following information was acquired from the responses to the Teacher Guide evaluation forms:

The majority of classes viewing "Carrascolendas" was composed of 81 to 100 percent Mexican-American pupils; only 9 percent had predominantly Anglo children in the classrooms. Three-fourths of the viewers were from kindergarten and first grades.

When questioned about the usefulness of the Guide, teachers responded positively. Coordination of suggestions with class activities received the least positive ratings, although concept learning was aided by Teacher Guide activities, with second-grade children profiting most. When asked to rate the various sections or features of the Guide, first- and second-grade teachers rated these features as more useful than did kindergarten teachers, although all ratings were positive. Music and translations of Spanish material appeared to be the most valuable portions of the Teacher Guide; self-concept activities, visuals, and capsule descriptions also received highly positive ratings.

When asked what changes they would make in the Teacher Guide, teachers gave the following responses:
1. Provide page numbers for each song, particularly for repetition of a song in a subsequent program.
2. Create a more detailed Teacher Guide.
3. Improve the lettering and the instructions for using visuals.
4. Give more explanation on historical and cultural points.
5. Combine suggestions for the use of visuals with the capsule description.
6. Provide names or page numbers for follow-up games and/or activities.
7. More English is needed; pronunciation of Spanish words would be very helpful.

Teachers indicated that the Guide was a great improvement over the previous year's supplementary guide and made very few suggestions for additions or changes. (Three-fourths of the teachers offered no

135

suggestions for improvements.) All suggestions concerning page number reorganization were carried out in the third-year Guide.

Since information regarding the Teacher Guide was incidentally mentioned in the program-by-program diaries during the first year, the detailed information obtained during the second year was very helpful. These previous results had indicated such positive response to the Guide that further reactions were requested on a smaller scale for the third year. The teacher questionnaire, discussed in Chapter 5 included questions regarding the clarity of the programs. Could the teachers deduce the behavioral objectives from the program itself, rather than depending on the Teacher Guide? In both the Texas and national response data, almost 90 percent of the teachers thought they could interpret the objectives. (This does not indicate, of course, how accurate they were.) In general, as can be seen below, results of the survey indicated that the Teacher Guide continued to be well received.

How often do you use the Teacher Guide?

Responses	Texas (N=196) March 1971	Texas (N=163) March 1972	Texas (N=290) Nov. 1972	National (N=86) Nov. 1972
Every program	1%	47%	22%	30%
Most programs	59	17	14	13
Some programs	13	17	30	11
Never	7	2	7	9
Do not have Teacher Guide	0	17	25	36
No response	20	0	2	1

How useful is the Teacher Guide?

Responses	Texas (N=196) March 1971	Texas (N=163) March 1972	Texas (N=290) Nov. 1972	National (N=86) Nov. 1972
Very useful	28%	58%	34%	28%
Somewhat useful	45	21	30	28
Not too useful	0	2	5	0
Useless	3	0	0	0
Do not have one	0	14	27	39
No response	24	5	4	5

The Teacher Guide for the series broadcast in 1973 differs from preceding ones in that it accompanies a new program series. Though new guides are necessary each year for the reedited series, many of the visuals can be reused from year to year.

The most recent Guide has many more suggestions for the children's participation as they view the program. The teachers may alert the children in advance of things to look for, building anticipation and attention. A chart of behavioral activities is added.

IN RETROSPECT

Had the project been able to devote a larger proportion of its funds to the development of the Teacher Guide, it would have been useful to have had detailed pilot testing and training of teachers in the use of the Guide. Ideally it would have been beneficial to provide an experimental "Carrascolendas" classroom as a proving ground for the educational activities included in the Guide and the series itself.

It is an interesting aside that some teachers used and benefited from the Guide, even though they and their children had no access to the television series. In a sense then, the Guide can stand alone.

In the view of the curriculum coordinator, the Guide was most effective in the areas of English and Spanish language skills and in history/culture. These areas also received the greatest emphasis in the television series. Suggestions for future improvement would be to develop a Visuals Kit in color and cardboard for greater eye appeal and durability. A multimedia approach would be helpful here; not only visuals but "tactiles" could be included for teachers and children to work with, emphasizing language teaching through behavior.

8

DISSEMINATION AND USAGE

One task in each year's evaluation of "Carrascolendas" was to identify the extent of its broadcast distribution and its viewer population. Although "Carrascolendas" was broadcast primarily on public television stations, and thus reached an audience larger than those of bilingual school children in their classes, our usage surveys focused on the school setting. This does not deny the importance of studying the extended usage of the program in private homes, particularly in the many cases where reruns of the series were made within the three years. However, the basic evaluation contract restricted our evaluation to the in-school audience.

The First Two Years

The first usage surveys were undertaken by mailing postcards to schools in the state of Texas. The postcard for the first year simply asked whether the school was using "Carrascolendas." In the second year it was more extensive; it included questions pertaining to the number of classes using the program, whether the respondents had heard about the series, and their reasons for not viewing it, if such was the case. In both years the return on the postcards (approximately 500 were sent in the first year; 750 in the second) was slightly less than 50 percent. In the first year approximately 37 percent of those schools returning the postcards were using the series. Of these, 35 percent had heard of it but were not using it, and 27 percent had not heard of it. In the second year percentages were roughly similar except there was a smaller percentage of schools who had never heard of the program. In both years, usage was heaviest by schools in the central area of Texas where promotion of the series by the regional service center had probably been the most concentrated and where the KLRN signal was best received. Typical reasons for not using the program were lack of an adequate television signal or the lack of Spanish instruction or related programs in the school's curricula. In the second year information was gathered on how respondents had learned of the program, and for the most part it was from information distributed by the Education Service Center.

One of the most important implications from the usage surveys of the first two years was that simple mailings and occasional publicity releases to the newspapers were insufficient to inform schools of the availability of "Carrascolendas." It probably can be assumed that most of the schools who had not responded to the survey—usually over 50 percent—had never heard of the series and were thus not motivated to return the postcard. (Some of our informal experience with such schools, such as when visitations were made in regard to other projects, revealed that particularly in the first year the effects of the promotional efforts for "Carrascolendas" were limited.) Those schools that used the program were typically ones that were engaged in some way in bilingual education. Usually a staff member had heard of the program through communication channels regarding bilingual education in the state of Texas or had been contacted through the Education Service Center.

The third year "Carrascolendas" was made available nationally as a series in the Public Broadcasting Service, which numbers 147 licensees with 233 transmitters. The survey was disseminated through mailing lists compiled from the Department of Health, Education, and Welfare Directory of Public Elementary and Secondary Schools in Selected Districts; this directory lists enrollment and staff by racial/ethnic group. The survey on which the directory was based includes the District of Columbia, but does not include Hawaii.

Forty-five public station licensees (31 percent of the national total) carried "Carrascolendas." Seven of these were not used in the evaluation because their states had less than 10 percent Spanish-surname children in the public schools. The locations of the remaining stations were:

State	No. of Stations	State	No. of Stations
Arizona	2	Michigan	4
California	6	Minnesota	1
Colorado	1	New Jersey	1
Connecticut	1	New Mexico	1

State	No. of Stations	State	No. of Stations
Florida	3	Ohio	2
Illinois	1	Pennsylvania	2
Kansas	1	Texas	5
Louisiana	1	Utah	1
Massachusetts	2	Washington	3
		Total	38

A major effort had been made to publicize the series nationally in the third year. Two thousand summary evaluation brochures were mailed by the Education Service Center to all bilingual directors, Title VII and Title I directors, state teachers' associations, state migrant directors, Catholic Diocese superintendents, Head Start and kindergarten state directors, and editors of Spanish-language newspapers. One thousand of the brochures were distributed by KLRN to all Public Broadcasting Service station managers, as well as to 82 newspapers and magazines.

The questionnaire for the third year's Usage Survey (sample copy in Appendix E) requested the following information: (1) number of classes in the different grade levels; the percentage of ethnic groups represented in the school; and whether they participated in a bilingual program, and were funded by Title VII or Title I; (2) availability of "Carrascolendas" and plans for viewing; (3) reasons for not viewing "Carrascolendas"; (4) how information about the series was first made available to the principal. Response to the survey was additionally encouraged by follow-up mailings to principals who had not returned the original survey sheet.

The characteristics of schools responding to the survey were indicated by the percentage of ethnic representation and the availability of bilingual programs at each school. Results are listed in Table 8.1 according to states. The national response was moderately good (29 percent). Ethnic percentages were broken down according to Mexican-American, black, Anglo, and other for tabulation. Only four states (Arizona, New Mexico, Oregon, and Texas) reported a majority of Mexican-Americans. All but three states (Kansas, Montana, and Wyoming) reported bilingual programs in 22 percent or more schools. On a national scale (N=1,502), 44 percent of the respondent schools participated in a bilingual program, 54 percent had no bilingual program, 2 percent gave no response.

"Carrascolendas" was available to 22 percent of the respondents but was not available at 352 schools (23 percent). Table 8.2 shows the comparison between states in terms of the availability of "Carrasco lendas." The largest response indicating program availability was from Texas with 202 schools responding positively. Texas accounts

Characteristics of the Respondent Schools

State*	Questionnaires Mailed N=5,279	Percentage Responding N=1,502	Percentage of Ethnicity of Respondents N=1,502 — Ethnic Groups				Percentage of Respondents Having Bilingual Programs N=1,502
			M-A	B	A	O	
Arizona	162	33%	40%	9%	34%	17%	44%
California	2,043	26	32	6	47	15	41
Colorado	247	33	36	5	46	13	3
Connecticut	78	28	7	37	24	32	64
Delaware	1	100					100
District of Columbia	2	50	30	30	30	10	100
Florida	131	35	6	24	35	35	65
Idaho	21	38	11	0	62	27	50
Illinois	165	29	25	18	30	27	62
Indiana	29	24	26	2	41	31	29
Iowa	6	67	16	5	55	24	50
Kansas	35	40	19	5	53	23	14
Louisiana	6	17	1	40	40	19	100
Maryland	4	50	0	27	17	56	50
Massachusetts	59	9	0	2	7	91	80
Michigan	84	20	20	9	55	16	24
Minnesota	9	44	22	1	32	45	75
Montana	5	40	26	6	19	49	0
Nebraska	12	17	30	0	67	3	50
Nevada	12	67	19	9	48	24	75
New Jersey	158	16	3	23	13	61	58
New Mexico	268	29	54	3	25	18	49
New York	420	4	1	38	13	48	75
Ohio	43	26	14	8	54	24	27
Oklahoma	11	27	14	15	69	2	33
Oregon	43	36	41	2	23	34	25
Pennsylvania	13	28	9	22	29	40	83
Rhode Island	1	100	0	44	56	0	100
Texas	1,081	41	50	7	30	13	44
Utah	38	61	24	4	54	18	22
Washington	40	20	33	0	50	17	50
Wisconsin	30	30	22	22	39	17	44
Wyoming	22	27	27	2	30	41	0

*States excluded did not have schools with 10 percent or more Spanish-surname children. (Alabama, Alaska, Arkansas, Georgia, Kentucky, Maine, Mississippi, Missouri, New Hampshire, North Carolina, North Dakota, South Carolina, South Dakota, Tennessee, Vermont, Virginia, and West Virginia.)

141

TABLE 8.2

Usage of "Carrascolendas"

State*	Number of Respondents N = 1,502	Number of Responses as to Availability of "Carrascolendas"				Number of Schools Viewing "Carrascolendas"			
		Yes	No	Don't Know	No Response	Yes	No	Don't Know	No Response
Arizona	54	8	13	33	0	6	22	24	2
California	539	50	123	358	8	55	161	299	24
Colorado	82	15	23	41	3	17	18	40	7
Connecticut	22	1	5	16	0	3	5	14	0
Delaware	1	0	0	1	0	0	1	0	0
District of Columbia	1	0	0	1	0	1	0	0	0
Florida	46	11	16	17	2	5	14	23	4
Idaho	8	2	2	4	0	3	1	4	0
Illinois	47	7	3	35	2	9	9	25	4
Indiana	7	0	3	4	0	0	2	4	1
Iowa	4	1	1	2	0	1	1	1	1
Kansas	14	0	5	7	2	1	3	9	1
Louisiana	1	1	0	0	0	0	1	0	0
Maryland	2	0	1	1	0	0	1	1	0
Massachusetts	5	0	1	4	0	0	1	4	0
Michigan	17	4	3	10	0	2	4	10	1
Minnesota	4	0	0	4	0	0	0	4	0
Montana	2	0	1	1	0	0	1	1	0
Nebraska	2	0	2	0	0	0	1	1	0
Nevada	8	6	2	0	0	1	3	4	0
New Jersey	26	1	7	18	0	9	1	14	2
New Mexico	77	14	33	28	2	17	18	35	7
New York	16	0	6	10	0	0	6	8	2
Ohio	11	2	3	6	0	0	2	9	0
Oklahoma	3	0	1	1	1	0	1	2	0
Oregon	4	4	0	0	0	2	1	1	0
Pennsylvania	12	1	4	7	0	1	2	8	1
Rhode Island	1	0	0	1	0	0	0	0	1
Texas	440	202	76	146	16	163	101	153	23
Utah	23	3	11	9	0	1	10	11	1
Washington	8	0	3	5	0	0	4	4	0
Wisconsin	9	3	1	5	0	1	2	5	1
Wyoming	6	1	3	2	0	0	4	2	0

*States excluded did not have schools with 10 percent or more Spanish-surname children. (Alabama, Alaska, Arkansas, Georgia, Kentucky, Maine, Mississippi, Missouri, New Hampshire, North Carolina, North Dakota, South Carolina, South Dakota, Tennessee, Vermont, Virginia, and West Virginia.)

for 13 percent of the 22 percent national response to availability of the series. Regarding plans for viewing "Carrascolendas," 50 percent responded in the "don't know" category. Over 25 percent of the respondents did not plan to view and 5 percent made no response. Of those respondents who knew that "Carrascolendas" was available in their area, 88 percent planned to view the series. In all, 20 percent of the national response indicated that they planned to view the series. From information requested about the sources from which schools learned about the series, results indicated approximately 21 percent had heard about it through school administrators or teachers. Results of the utilization survey bear out the fact that, though publicity was greatly increased from that of preceding years, the available viewing audience is still not adequately informed. However, in Texas, viewing has increased as a direct result of publicity and teacher workshops in the KLRN viewing area.

MANAGEMENT EVALUATION

A process evaluation of management was undertaken to give an account of the way "Carrascolendas" was developed and to serve as input for future efforts. The processes that contributed to the final product include the project components, the schedule, and information feedback in the management structure.

Program Development

The continuous stream of coordination and interaction is depicted in the flowchart (Figure 8.1) whose starting point was the preparation of content areas and behavioral objectives. Every aspect of the program development emphasized the Mexican-American culture and heritage. The success of the feedback process depended on firm scheduling. Initially the project was hampered by a late start in curriculum development; this resulted in little or no time for script critiques by the curriculum staff and advisory committee. Initially many of the suggestions of the evaluation team could not be implemented because pertinent segments had already been videotaped. In scheduling it was found that much more time was needed between the production staff's receipt of content and objectives and the videotaping of that particular program. This would allow the existing feedback mechanisms to function more effectively.

FIGURE 8.1

PROGRAM DEVELOPMENT PROCESS

FIGURE 8.1

PROGRAM DEVELOPMENT PROCESS

144

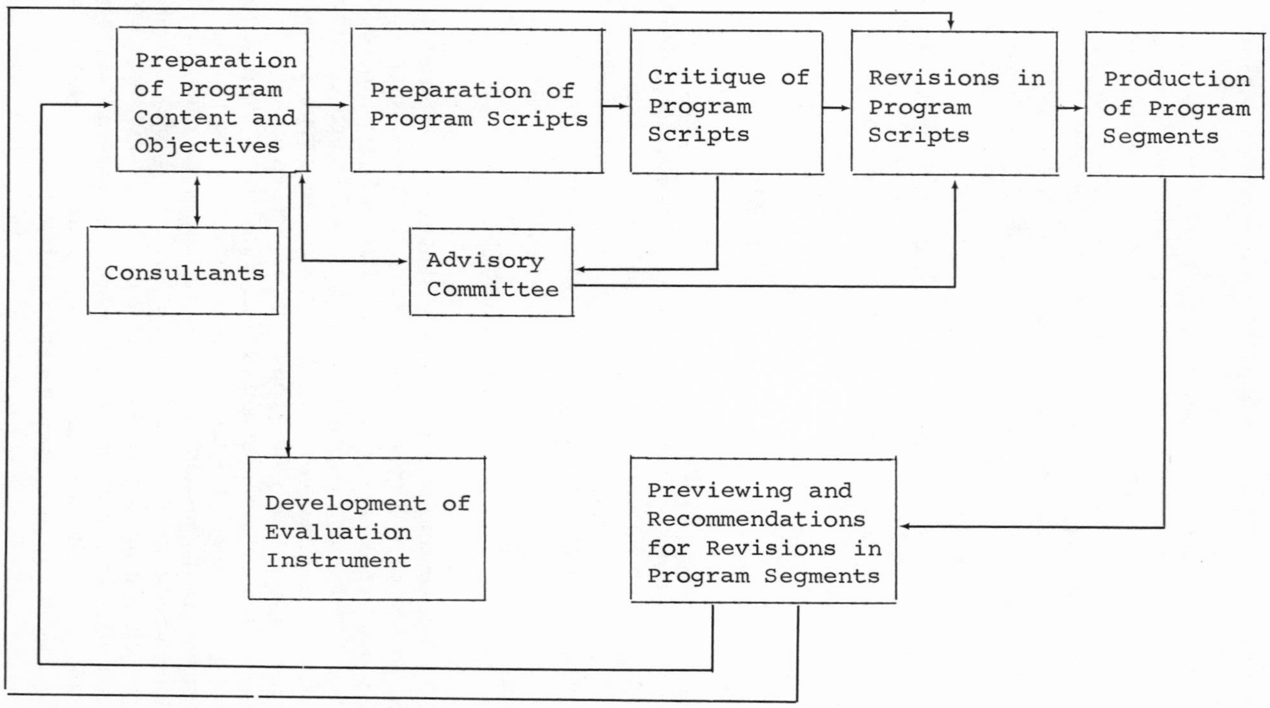

Staff Organization

As was mentioned in Chapter 1, the "Carrascolendas" project
operated administratively under the principal contractor, Education
Service Center, Region XIII, Austin, Texas. The project was represented in the Service Center by the television coordinator. Within
the Center, the television coordinator was assisted by a curriculum
coordinator whose task was to prepare the behavioral objectives for
the program.

Four components outside of the regional service center comprised the additional management organization of the project. The
major of these was KLRN-TV which had the subcontract to produce
the series. The activities of this component were under the direction
of the executive producer. Another major subcontractor in the project
was the Center for Communication Research, which carried out the
independent evaluations of the series. An independent advisory board
made up of citizens from the community and leaders in bilingual education was to promote the link between the project and the community.
Finally, there was a minor component, labeled "independent educational
audit," that was to review the work of the evaluators and to report as
its label implies. In the main, however, the major components of the
project were the Education Service Center with the television coordinator and curriculum coordinator, the executive producer who headed
KLRN-TV's activities, and the evaluation team. In the final year of
the project, a field relations coordinator was added to the staff of the
Service Center to promote usage of the series in the schools. The
role delineation of these management components is summarized in
Table 8.3.

Over the three years of the project some problems arose as to
the division of the duties assigned to the various management components. It was often difficult for the television and curriculum coordi-
nators to plan sufficiently far ahead so that behavioral objectives
could be carefully reviewed by the evaluators and the executive producer prior to the latter engaging in script preparation activities.
Part of this problem was due to the unfamiliarity of the basic staff
members with the concept of behavioral objectives and the time taken
for them to learn the uses of them. The television coordinator also
had a major problem in his first year in adhering to the project schedule since the project was late in starting and activities many times
had to be accelerated in order to meet an air date of the first of the
new year. There was also a basic problem in effective coordination
between the Education Service Center personnel and the television
production personnel. The physical separation of these components
by some five miles was one communication problem. The other was
an agreement upon the level of communication that would not be assumed

145

TABLE 8.3

Summary of Major Staff Positions

Position	Description
Television Coordinator	insures that project activities are compatible with state and federal policy; secures services of consultants; coordinates public relations activities; serves as liaison between research and production components.
Curriculum Coordinator	develops objectives, content, and Teacher Guide materials; assesses suitability of materials and programs through direct contact with children in classrooms.
Executive Producer	designs and coordinates the series and in-service programs; assumes responsibility for all aspects of production, hiring and directing personnel; reports on activities to the Education Service Center, the Office of Education, the Advisory Board, and the evaluation team.
Advisory Board	provides suggestions and criticisms in the areas of obtaining consultants, formulating objectives and content, utilizing appropriate television techniques, developing workshops, and encouraging community involvement and program utilization.
Evaluation Team	prepares evaluation design and instrumentation; engages in school liaison activities; pre- and posttests target population; conducts surveys and formative evaluations; submits a final report of the evaluation.
Field Relations Coordinator	establishes field relations and coordination of test sites; organizes and conducts in-service sessions; disseminates information and supplementary materials. (This position was included for the third year only.)

to connote interference of the educational planners with the creative aspects of the production process. After a number of communication problems along this line in the first year, regular weekly meetings were scheduled along with the evaluators and this seemed to smooth out the schedule somewhat.

However, these foregoing types of problems, which can be found in any project, did not hamper the personnel from essentially fulfilling their assignments during the three years of the project and increasing considerably in efficiency in each year. In short, the aims of the project were carried out quite well, and the foregoing criticisms are meant to guide future projects rather than to reflect negatively upon this project. The advice for future projects is that care be taken initially to be sure that all personnel concerned understand the concept of behavioral objectives and that the time necessary for the development of such objectives and their refinement be incorporated into the developmental schedule.

The advisory board, a component that is deemed particularly important in bicultural education and Title VII activities, essentially was nonfunctional in the present project. Several of the persons on the board were very active and could often be called upon for advice, including the chairman of the group. On the other hand, it was very difficult to call the entire group together because most of the personnel were very much involved in other community and educational activities. When a meeting was called, it was difficult to ask for more time from any individual than he was spending simply in attending the meeting. It is highly recommended that if the advisory-board concept is to work, then funds must be made available to compensate persons for their time on the project. This would place the chairman of such a committee in a position where he could reasonably ask for more in the way of obligations of time and energy from board members.

The position of field relations coordinator was established in the third year of the project in order to facilitate dissemination of information and to encourage schools to use the series. For the most part, this position was potentially an effective one, and for workshops that were held, the response was favorable. Perhaps the largest problem in the duties of the field relations coordinator was the national dissemination of information on the project. There was a considerable shortcoming in terms of schools in the United States that had bilingual programs but that still had not heard of "Carrascolendas." It is probably very important that in future projects of national scope, a national information campaign be organized, and that professional help be enlisted for same. This would include newspaper publicity campaigns, advertising campaigns, and perhaps in the case of educational television, promotional spots on both commercial and educational networks. The field relations coordinator should be a person who has some background in public information campaigns.

SUMMARY

In retrospect it was considered quite useful that the evaluation component of "Carrascolendas" did require attention given to project management, although it must be admitted that these activities were not given high priority. Utilization surveys definitely indicated that a major challenge of a project of this type is simply to reach potential users of the television product. While it may be admirable to create an excellent television series and to make it available, a project is still only as successful as it can encourage people to use its product. In brief, the utilization surveys loomed more important in retrospect because they consistently indicated a weakness in the promotional efforts of the "Carrascolendas" project.

While the technical reports of the project present more detailed information on role delineation of the different positions and their evolution over the three years of the project, Table 8.3 provides a useful guide for further television projects. If a project is a joint effort, such as this one, between an educational organization and a television station, then positions of television coordinator and executiv producer should be useful. On the other hand, if a project does not have to bridge two organizations, then it is probably important that one senior position be developed, probably that of executive producer, and all supervision of project management be delegated to the person in this position. This means, however, that the executive producer, unlike in the present project, would probably not have the time to engage in scriptwriting or playing a role in the series.

9

During the course of the project, various questions arose that led us to conduct studies relevant to the project, but not in the mainstream of the evaluation. In this chapter we will present the highlights of some of these studies with the twofold purpose of adding information to the topic of bilingual education through television, while at the same time providing examples of types of research strategies that may be useful for future projects. The most important of these studies, a self-concept measure, will be explained in greater detail. These studies were:

1. Formative studies: Children's reactions to film narrations and art and music styles were studied to determine the most effective method of presentation.

2. Child attitude surveys: The aim was to elicit children's subjective reactions to the television series as well as information on their attitudes toward television as a whole.

3. Parent attitude surveys: The objective was to secure information from adults and parents in the community about their attitude toward the "Carrascolendas" series.

4. Effects of teacher bilingualism: A further analysis was made of the teacher attitude surveys in order to determine whether the degree of the teacher's bilingualism was related to her attitudes toward the program.

5. Relations of children's language dominance to learning gains: The question was answered whether the effects of "Carrascolendas" might be tied to the Mexican-American child's basic ability to speak English or Spanish or both.

6. Self-concept measures: The question was whether the program might have effects upon measures of self-concept that were closer to the conceptual definitions than were many of the specific behavioral objectives in the self-concept area.

AN EXAMPLE OF FORMATIVE EVALUATIONS

Although formative evaluation did not receive emphasis in the contracts under which the evaluations were conducted, there were times when we were asked to "pretest" a particular segment, topic, or media technique. This was to help the production staff make decisions concerning those items.

Essentially, formative evaluations involve taking small samples of materials out into the field and testing them with groups of children. In most cases our research strategies were rather simple, and the results were usually tabulated on the spot, so that interpretations could be furnished rapidly to the program producers. One of several formative studies done over the three years, this particular study included a comparison of film segments with different types of narration as well as assessment of the children's preferences for different styles of music and art. In order to illustrate the kinds of strategies undertaken in the formative study, rather than all the detailed results, we will concentrate on the study of the art materials in this discussion.

The essential question in the art study was that of assessing responses to three radically different styles including: op-art, where the presentation is relatively abstract; Disney-like art, where the subject is treated in a cartoon style; and realistic art, where the topic is presented in a straightforward, descriptive way. Three different objects were presented—a horse, a house, and a rooster—in each style. Test materials were developed that represented every combination of the three art styles with the three subjects.

The questions in this case referred both to the children's expressed preferences for the different art styles as well as their ability to recognize the subjects presented in a particular art style.

We used two types of attitude measures. One was an attitude scale presenting a continuum of faces ranging from a pronounced frown to a pronounced smile, as shown in Figure 9.1.

FIGURE 9.1

Pictorial Attitude Measure

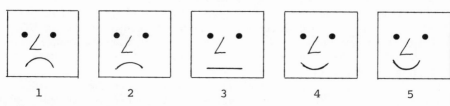

This type of attitude measure can be used with relatively young children and the validity of its use can be readily checked. In the present case validity was assessed by asking children several questions for which we would anticipate quite different responses on the scale, such as "How do you feel about eating candy?" Or "How do you feel about getting a spanking?" It is also easy to check on reliability of responses simply by repeating a question occasionally to children and seeing the degree to which the responses are the same. In the present case we took informal tests along these lines as sufficient evidence of validity and reliability of the scale. A child's preference was additionally indexed by presenting him with several of the pictures and asking him to mark the one which he liked the best of those before him. Finally, comprehension of the art presentations was assessed by presenting the child with a picture, then asking him: "Can you tell me what this picture is?" Responses were then scored as right or wrong.

The children who participated in the art study (and also the film and music preference studies) were 90 Mexican-American kindergarten, first-, and second-grade students in a San Antonio school. It was possible to test the children in six groups of 15; each group contained five children from each grade level.

We calculated "preference" scores by assigning numbers to the steps on the scale, ranging from "one" (distinct frown) to "five" (distinct smile). The results of the analysis of the attitude measures indicated that the children favored particular combinations of styles and topics. Thus, for example, the op-art style was preferred for the house (69 percent) as against the Disney-like (20 percent) and realistic (11 percent) styles. Similar results were found in response to the rooster where 56 percent preferred the op-art style when compared to the Disney-like (41 percent) and realistic (3 percent) styles. However, the Disney-like style (45 percent) was best liked for the horse rather than the op-art (40 percent) and realistic (11 percent) styles.

Our analysis of the children's ability to recognize items portrayed in the art work indicated further differences. When objects were portrayed in the op-art style, the pictures elicited a significantly lower recognition score (59 percent) than when objects were portrayed in the other two styles (Disney-like, 93 percent, and realistic, 98 percent). Thus, the producer was faced with something of a dilemma. The children were more attracted to the op-art style, but it was the op-art style that might result in the most confusion about what the object to be illustrated actually was.

The present study is summarized, not so much to indicate conclusions about art styles, but to illustrate how simple scaling procedures and questions of recognition could yield objective data on children's responses. Such data are better than simply "trying out"

segments and leaving the conclusions to the subjective observations
of the researchers or the producer. Given some further attention,
the simple design in the present example could be expanded into a
comprehensive study.

SURVEY OF CHILDREN'S ATTITUDES

Another study that proved extremely useful during the project was
a direct survey of the children, not only for information on their reactions to "Carrascolendas," but for other relevant attitudes such as
feelings about different kinds of television programs, watching television in school, and a variety of items related to Mexican-American
life. Our experience indicated that questions on these topics were
best presented in a multiple-choice format. Since the survey for the
third year involved a refined questionnaire as well as results from
different parts of the United States, this study is summarized here.

In the third year the Child Attitude Survey consisted of 17
multiple-choice or yes-no questions (Appendix F) presented as soon
as the English posttest was concluded. Forty-eight children were
scheduled to be interviewed at each site, including viewer and nonviewer children from kindergarten, first, and second grades. Response
data were obtained from all of the national test sites including a group
of third graders from Pueblo. A total of 544 interviews were tabulated.

We found that overall responses to the Child Attitude Survey
were positive. A large majority of the children watched television at
home and also enjoyed watching at school. Respondents indicated that
they liked bilingual television shows (Spanish and English). However,
children generally spoke English to their peers (67 percent), parents
(51 percent), siblings (62 percent), and teachers (73 percent), although
at some sites Spanish, or Spanish and English, was used to a great
extent when children spoke to their parents.

The children who were viewing "Carrascolendas" (420) generally
liked the series very much. They understood the Spanish segments
(60 percent) presented in the programs and understood the English
segments (87 percent) to an even greater extent.

Participation in repeating the words flashed on the television
as well as in singing the songs was very good. Over two-thirds of
the children who viewed participated. A large percentage of the
respondents (89 percent) indicated that they liked the songs; approximately one-third could sing one of the songs learned from "Carrascolendas."

SURVEYS OF PARENTAL ATTITUDES

In the second year of the project, an attempt was made to survey systematically parents of children who were in a test-site school. Results of these surveys indicated the degree to which "Carrascolendas" had become known by the parents and what their attitudes were toward it. Other questions in the survey of interest to us were those that revealed parents' attitudes about bilingual education. The results of the Parent Attitude Survey undertaken at the national test sites in the third year are presented in this section, since they illustrate our best-developed techniques for such surveys and some of the attitudes we found in different parts of the United States.

Parents' attitudes were assessed by means of a telephone survey that was conducted in either Spanish or English, depending on the language preferred by the person interviewed. A list of parents with Spanish surnames was obtained from two elementary schools in Austin during the second year. The results measured the responses of 100 people contacted who had children viewing "Carrascolendas." The survey showed that parents had learned of the program through their children, and approximately one-third of those parents watched "Carrascolendas." The parents liked the sections on Mexican customs and felt that their children's knowledge of Spanish had improved through viewing "Carrascolendas."

In the national study it was decided that a random sample of parents' names would be obtained from each test-site school. The population would not necessarily be limited to people with Spanish surnames. Percentages of Mexican-American parents in the schools at each site averaged approximately 92 percent, except for Lansing and Tracy, which averaged 27 percent. Bilingual interviewers again assessed parents' attitudes by means of a telephone survey. These interviews took place during the months when "Carrascolendas" was being aired at each test site.

The survey instrument (Appendix G) was designed for parents having children who viewed television. If a person contacted had no children or no television set, he/she was not interviewed. The instrument provided possible response categories to every question in order to facilitate procedures for the interviewer. A response category marked "other" was provided with space for comments elicited from the parent when their responses were not included in the response categories. The instrument was designed to allow the person interviewed to respond in both a positive and a negative manner to the same question; that is, "Yes, bilingual programs are good for teaching Spanish, but they take up too much school time."

The attitudes of parents were assessed in two ways: (1) opinions regarding bilingual television programs and the use of one or more languages; (2) opinions regarding "Carrascolendas" and its features, if the parent had viewed one or more programs.

One hundred parents were to be interviewed at each site. However, the number of completed and correctly scored interviews varied from site to site, eventually yielding a total of 688 responses.

The Parent Attitude Survey indicated that over half of the parents knew their children viewed "Carrascolendas" at school, at home, or at both places.

Responses to the importance of a bilingual television series for primary school children were favorable, and at all sites the majority of respondents preferred that their children speak both Spanish and English. The teaching of Mexican-American customs was deemed important and very few negative responses were elicited.

Almost two-thirds of the respondents had never viewed the series and did not respond to the questions dealing with particular aspects of "Carrascolendas." Of the remaining third, parents generally learned about the program through information provided by the school, on television, and by their children.

In those categories where both positive and negative comments were elicited, responses were generally positive toward the series. Responses to likes and dislikes of the series were favorable. The majority of respondents felt that "Carrascolendas" was a good program and that the Mexican customs presented in the series were well done. Ninety percent of the parents liked the Spanish used in the programs, and many felt that the children had profited by learning both Spanish and English, but particularly Spanish.

Few changes were suggested, although more exposure to Spanish was cited often (32 percent). Parents felt that the series had helped their children develop pride in their Mexican-American culture, mentioning improvement in Spanish as a secondary effect of viewing.

RELATIONS BETWEEN TEACHER BILINGUALISM
IN SPANISH AND ENGLISH AND ATTITUDES
TOWARD "CARRASCOLENDAS"

During the second year of the project, the practical question was raised as to whether a teacher's Spanish-language abilities were related in any way to her use of, or attitudes toward, "Carrascolendas." Several visits to schools had shown this to be a frequent topic of inquiry, and it had practical ramifications when it came to considering if "Carrascolendas" could be used by a teacher who had no knowledge of Spanish. Since all teachers spoke English, the Spanish-language ability was also an index of bilingualism. The development of the program and the Teacher Guide had been based on the assumption that the program would be successful no matter what language abilities the teacher had. In fact, it was assumed that the program would have a realistic secondary audience of children who would watch it outside of the school environment. On the other hand, evaluations of "Sesame Street" and the ongoing evaluations of "Carrascolendas" pointed to the importance of supplementary activities in increasing a program's impact upon children.

We approached the question of the possible relationship of teacher bilingualism to use of the program in the second year's study by taking teacher attitude questionnaires and differentiating them in terms of the teachers' responses to the question, "How well do you speak Spanish?" We looked for a relationship between the response to this item and the responses to other items on the questionnaire. This relationship could be explored statistically* to provide us with an indication of what kinds of teacher attitudes and practices concerning the program might be related to teacher bilingualism.

The questionnaire used in this study was the same as the one described earlier in Chapter 5 for the second year's evaluation (Appendix C). The assessment of teachers' responses to the language question indicated a fairly diverse distribution across the different response categories.

How well do you speak Spanish?

	Number	Percent
Fluently	49	29
Moderately	39	23
Limitedly	44	26
Not bilingual	39	23
Total	171	100

Given the identification of responses in these categories, the questionnaire results were then cross-tabulated for each of the other items; a statistical index was calculated to determine the degree to which there was a relationship beyond chance between the teacher's language ability in Spanish and her responses to other portions of the questionnaire.

Probably the most practical finding of this ad hoc study was that use of, and attitudes toward, the program are for the most part

---

*By the use of Chi-Square it was possible to identify if the relations between teacher language ability and responses to various questions went beyond what might occur by chance alone.

155

independent of degree of teacher bilingualism. One artifact of the study was that teachers who tended to be more fluent in Spanish also had more Mexican-American children in class. This was the cause of other relationships between teacher fluency in Spanish and children's ability to speak Spanish in class, viewing "Carrascolendas" previously, and the like. There was also a somewhat lower frequency of Spanish-speaking teachers in kindergarten; this may have been a reflection of the recent organization of kindergartens in the state of Texas.

Probably the most important relationship with teacher fluency in Spanish was the tendency to conduct more classroom activities in conjunction with the program and the reported ability to perceive the behavioral objectives in the program segments. Thus while teacher bilingualism may not have been necessary for the children to react to the program per se, the teacher's ability to speak Spanish may have been an important tool relative to pupil gains. This cluster of relationships also included the somewhat more favorable responses of Spanish-speaking teachers to the language and cultural-historical materials of the series, and teacher observation of more Spanish speaking by pupils as a function of viewing the series. This, of course, could be tied to the greater amount of classroom activities conducted by the Spanish-speaking teacher.

From a policy implication standpoint, it seemed clear that the use of "Carrascolendas" in the classroom does not depend upon having a bilingual teacher, but the supplementary activities that accompany the series may be more effectively implemented by a Spanish-speaking teacher.

ARE LEARNING GAINS RELATED TO THE
CHILDREN'S LANGUAGE DOMINANCE?

Although all of the children included in the evaluation components of "Carrascolendas were Mexican-American and were assumed to be bilingual to some degree, there was considerable variation among the children in terms of being Spanish dominant, English dominant, or completely bilingual. Children's language dominance as a factor influencing the learning gains resulting from viewing the program was questioned. At the conclusion of our second year's evaluation of the project, we tried to answer this question formally by making further analyses of the evaluation data. We are including this study in the present volume because it illustrates simple methods for assessing a child's linguistic dominance and the relative independence of learning gains from such dominance.

We needed a valid index of language dominance and were unable to conduct detailed linguistic field interviews with children to determine such dominance. As a consequence, we settled on two measures, were able to check one against the other, and thus gained confidence in their validity. One such measure was simply the teacher's rating of a child as either English dominant, Spanish dominant, or completely bilingual. The second index of language dominance was based upon our fieldworkers' ratings of the children's fluency as they answered questions. Some questions were meant to elicit a continuous response from the child, that is, several words or complete sentences; the fieldworker scored the child's response on a one-to-four fluency scale. By comparing ratings for questions on Spanish items with those on English items, it was possible to compute the child's average fluency rating when he operated in these two languages during the interviews.

We would expect that, if our two different ratings of linguistic ability were accurate, they should agree with one another. Such a comparison was made, and it was clear that the two measures reflected one another to a substantial degree. For example, it was found that children whose teachers classified them as Spanish dominant had a higher average fluency score on Spanish items (2.00) than on English items (1.45). As expected, children who were rated English dominant had higher fluency scores on English items (2.26) than on Spanish items (0.72). A comparison of these two types of dominance, in terms of fluency ratings, suggested that children who are English dominant were not fluent in Spanish; whereas children who were fluent in Spanish had some degree of fluency in English. We would expect fluency ratings for the children who had been classified as bilingual by their teachers to be quite similar in both Spanish and English. Indeed, they were; their average fluency in Spanish was 1.90, as against 2.08 in English.

Among the measures of learning gains in the second year were children's average scores on a one-to-four scale of correctness in response to the test items. One way of determining whether learning gains were related to language dominance or fluency was to calculate statistical coefficients of correlation, where .00 indicates no correlation, larger than .05 indicates more than a chance relationship, and indexes above .50 could be interpreted as a degree of relationship that was of interest to us. We wanted to discover whether statistically significant relationships existed between learning gains in Spanish or English and (1) whether the child viewed the program, (2) whether he viewed the program and had activities, (3) whether he was bilingual, (4) whether he was English dominant, (5) whether he was Spanish dominant, (6) his average rating of fluency in English, and (7) his average rating of fluency in Spanish.

There was only a small degree of relationship between the child's viewing the program and his gain scores in the Spanish area. We found this relationship too small to be interpreted with confidence.

By contrast, both the viewing and the activities were moderately, to highly, related with gain scores in English. Such results reflected what was reported in Chapter 3. That is, viewing the program had more effects on gains in English than in Spanish.

What is particularly important, however, is that none of the correlation coefficients between the teacher classifications of the child's language dominance or our ratings of fluency indicated a relationship with gain scores in Spanish or English. Thus it can be concluded quite definitely that there was no, or nothing more than a negligible, relationship between a child's language dominance and gain scores in the Spanish or English test areas.

SELF-CONCEPT MEASURES

Among all the objectives of the "Carrascolendas" series, those focusing on the self-concept of the Mexican-American child were not only perhaps the most important, but also those that promised to benefit the most from televised instruction. Ironically, it was the measures of self-concept, by being tied to detailed behavioral objectives of the program, that were often criticized because they did not directly reflect conceptual definitions of self-concept. Examples of these objectives are that the child will (1) know that he helps other people, (2) be able to identify the nuclear family, and (3) know that he speaks two languages.

Although the use of criterion-referenced measures is justifiable in the context of measuring specified objectives, are such measures generalizable to more conceptual definitions of self-concept? This summary describes the development and pilot testing of an instrument based on conceptual definitions of self-concept and applied to children in the "Carrascolendas" project.

A review of the literature indicates that conceptual definitions of self-concept usually account for at least two factors: (1) the identification or perception of self-attributes, and (2) the evaluation of self-attributes. Alan Coller presents a comprehensive state-of-the-art report on the definition and measurement of self-concept in early childhood. Some of the representative conceptual definitions cited are.[1]

Coller: self-concept is an organized collection of attitudes, beliefs, and feelings a person has about himself.

Raimy: a more or less perceptual object resulting from present and past self-observation; self-concept is a "map which each person consults in order to understand himself, especially during moments of crisis or choice."

<u>Perkins:</u> perception, beliefs, feelings, and values that one finds
      descriptive of himself.
<u>Strong and Feder:</u> every evaluation statement a person makes about
      himself is a sample of his self-concept.
<u>Rogers:</u> self as an explanatory concept is the organized, consistent,
      conceptual gestalt composed of perceptions of the characteristics
      of "I" and "me" and perceptions of relationships of I and me
      to others and to various aspects of life.

These conceptualizations reflect the perceptual and evaluative
dimensions in self-concept. Rogers' definition reflects the variation
that may occur in self-concept due to situational effects. In other
words, one may generally have a high self-concept, but in a particular
social situation one might have a low self-concept because of the
social variables of that situation. This could be a confounding variable,
if not controlled, in the measurement of self-concept. In particular,
when dealing with subjects from a bicultural environment, the variable
of culture might be an especially salient component of the social situation. Cultural awareness, for example, may have a significant effect
on both perception and evaluation of self-attributes.

A test instrument was developed for pilot use with the posttest
in the "Carrascolendas" third-year evaluation. Thirty-nine items
were developed for formative testing. The formative testing involved
the use of a separate 92-subject sample of Mexican-American (the
target audience) and Anglo first and second graders from Albuquerque.

From the formative testing a pool of items was developed that
would reflect the following facets of self-concept:
1. perception of self-attributes;
2. evaluation of self-attributes when one considers oneself in isola-
    tion;
3. evaluation of self-attributes when one considers oneself in various
    social situations, including (a) home, (b) classroom, and (c)
    peer group; and
4. evaluation of self-attributes that may be related to cultural dif-
    ferences.

Items were constructed to measure these four elements. After
reviewing the initial pool of items, 39 items were selected that appeared to have high validity for measurement of the perceptual and
evaluative dimensions of self-concept. A list of these items is provided
in Appendix H. Of the 39 items, six were designed to elicit responses
regarding perception of self-attributes (items one-six). The remaining 33 items were designed to elicit evaluative responses. A simple
yes-no answer was requested on the first six items and a five-point
pictorial attitude measure was used to elicit responses on the 33
evaluative items. For example, the child was asked, "Can you do one
thing nobody else can do?" The response to this item was yes or no;

it was assumed that a high percentage of yes responses would indicate that subjects in the sample population could conceive of themselves as individuals apart from various social units. An example of an evaluative item is, "When you look at yourself in the mirror, how do you feel?" This was constructed to measure self-concept when the child considers himself in isolation, apart from any social unit. An example of the questions designed to measure how the child evaluates himself in various social units is, "When your teacher asks you a question and you don't know the answer, how do you feel?" The instrument was administered bilingually (in Spanish and English) to encourage maximum response.

Results of the perception items of the formative test revealed that children in the target audience did perceive self-attributes in a meaningful way. The percentage of yes and no responses to each of the first six items is shown in Table 9.1.

Responses to all 39 items were analyzed in an effort to (1) determine whether the 39 items tapped dimensions related to the conceptual definitions of self-concept, and (2) determine whether the total number of scales could be reduced, so that a shorter test instrument could be used in field experiment posttesting. Factor analysis was useful in answering both questions.

Factor analysis revealed that over half of the 39 items clustered in four groups, or "factors," of five items each. We selected most of the items for the pilot test instrument from the four major groups, choosing items with the highest correlations in each group. Items that were linguistically oriented were selected as pairs for both Spanish and English. For example, if an item regarding hearing parents speak

TABLE 9.1

Responses to Perception Items on Formative Test
of Self-Concept

Item Number	Percent Responding "YES"	Percent Responding "NO"
1. Make yourself a sandwich	88	12
2. Something yours, no one else's	80	20
3. Talking to puppy in Spanish	19	81
4. Visit friend by yourself	66	34
5. Do something nobody else can	66	34
6. Find food on deserted island	31	69

Spanish was selected, then the item regarding hearing parents speak
English was also selected to maintain linguistic pairing of items.
The ten items selected are summarized in abbreviated form below:

1. Hearing parents speak English
2. Teacher happy with school work
3. You talking in Spanish
4. Playing like a grown-up
5. Playing with Spanish-speaking friend
6. Hearing parents speak Spanish
7. Something yours, no one else's
8. You talking in English
9. Parents happy with school work
10. Playing with English-speaking friend

The resulting ten-item pilot instrument included items concerned
with the social situation of the classroom, the home, and the peer
group. These items fulfilled the first requirement of a test instrument related to the conceptual definition of self-concept. The second
requirement, that the test be sensitive to cultural differences, was
also fulfilled by including paired items where each item was repeated
for both Spanish and English. For example, the child was asked how
he felt when he heard his parents speak English and when he heard
his parents speak Spanish. Only evaluative items were included in the
pilot test instrument.

The ten-item test instrument was administered in both Spanish
and English to all subjects in the field experiment immediately following the Spanish posttest. The test administrator read each of the test
items and asked the child to mark how he felt about each item on the
five-scale pictorial attitude measure (see Figure 9.1).

The primary question of interest was whether or not a test of
self-concept based on conceptual definitions would discriminate viewers
from nonviewers in the "Carrascolendas" field experiment sample
population.

In order to determine whether or not the test of self-concept
discriminated viewers from nonviewers, the mean score of each group
on each item in the test was statistically compared. These comparisons
revealed no significant differences in the mean scores of viewers
contrasted with nonviewers on any single item. Similar comparisons
were made of viewers and nonviewers at each grade level. Again the
comparisons revealed no significant differences between viewers and
nonviewers at any one grade level.

Although none of the test items, when considered individually,
discriminated viewers from nonviewers, it was possible that some
group or combination of items would discriminate. In order to determine if any group of items would discriminate viewers from nonviewers, responses were subjected to multiple discriminate analysis.

This technique enables the researcher to discover if any subset of items, taken in combination, significantly discriminates viewers from nonviewers, or if the total test significantly discriminates viewers from nonviewers. When viewers and nonviewers from all three grades were combined, the multiple discriminate analysis revealed that no combination of test items significantly discriminated viewers from nonviewers.

The results of the analysis of responses of the self-concept test instrument indicated that none of the items alone, or in combination, significantly differentiated between viewers and nonviewers. These results are not too surprising when it is considered that the pilot test instrument was based upon conceptual definitions of self-concept, which encompass a rather global view. A stimulus such as the "Carrascolendas" program series that occupies a very small percentage of the child's daily life could not be expected realistically to have a significant impact on a personality trait defined in such a comprehensive manner. This would be analogous to expecting the effects of a breakfast program for children to have marked effects upon their physical growth within a very short period of time, where perhaps no other nutritional factors were varied.

NOTE

1. Alan R. Coller, The Assessment of "Self Concept" in Early Childhood Education, Rev. Ed. ERIC ED 057 910 (July 1971); V. C. Raimy, "Self-reference in Counseling Interviews," Journal of Consulting Psychology 12 (1948): 155; H. V. Perkins, "Factors Influencing Change in Children's Self Concept," Child Development 29 (1958): 221-30; D. Strong and D. Feder, "Measurement of the Self-Concept: A Critique of the Literature," Journal of Consulting Psychology 8 (1961): 170-78; C. R. Rogers, Client-Centered Therapy (Boston: Houghton Mifflin, 1951).

10

TOWARD CULTURALLY
TARGETED EDUCATIONAL
TELEVISION

Although most of this book has been devoted to the details of "Carrascolendas," in this chapter we will try to draw some generalizations that go beyond this particular project and that we hope will guide others in what we call culturally targeted educational television.

"CARRASCOLENDAS": THREE YEARS' EVALUATION IN RETROSPECT

The most concise way to summarize the results of the three years' evaluation is given in Table 10.1, which indicates for grade levels and areas of behavioral objectives those instances where viewer gains statistically exceeded those of nonviewers in our measurements. Based upon the detailed findings reported in Chapters 3 and 4, as well as the results summarized in Table 10.1, we have formulated the following generalizations:
1. Gains were observed in the English area of history/culture for all three years.
2. Third-year gains were seen for first graders in four of the five Spanish areas and for kindergartners in three of the five English areas.
3. Both Spanish and English language skill gains were apparent in the second and third years.
4. Least effects were noted in the second grade (except for the English area of history/culture).

Attitudes

Various attitudinal measures were not only useful for overall evaluation, but for suggesting feedback to the programs' producers

TABLE 10.1

Viewer Gains Across Three Years

	First Year			Second Year	Third Year			
Spanish Areas	First Grade	Second Grade	Combined Grades	First Grade Only	Kinder-garten	First Grade	Second Grade	Combined Grades
History/Culture					*		*	*
Self-Concept						*		
Science							*	*
Math				*		*		*
Language Skills				*		*		
Phoneme/Grapheme								
Total Areas								
English Areas								
History/Culture (Multicultural social environment)[1]		*		*		*		*
Self-Concept				*	*			
Science (Physical environment)			*		*		*	*
Language Skills			*	*	*	*		*
Math[2] (Cognitive development)			*	*			*	*
Total Areas			*					

Key

*Significant difference (p < .05).

[1]The areas denoted in parentheses were labeled in that way only during the first year.

[2]Although treated exclusively in Spanish, Math was tested in English during the second year.

and to the schools. Generalizations about these attitudes are as follows:

1. Teacher Attitude Questionnaires consistently revealed that a high proportion of Mexican-American children felt proud, or at least accepting, of their cultural heritage;

the program was thought to increase self-esteem;

the Teacher Guide encouraged the implementation of, and increased participation in, supplementary class activities;

English-speaking children benefited by learning some Spanish and by becoming interested in another culture;

the series was thought to be excellent in developing both Spanish and English language skills;

teachers judged the level of material to be appropriate for their students;

animation was highly rated for entertainment value and as an instructional technique;

the program was very popular;

some segments incorporated too much repetition;

vocabulary should relate more pertinently to the home and community;

most of the program seemed to be academically geared toward first grade.

2. Teacher Diaries on a program-by-program basis revealed that

songs and animation were the most popular production techniques;

Agapito (the lion) was a favorite character throughout the series;

the more amusing segments, regardless of characters, had high appeal;

children were encouraged to have more pride in their native tongue and culture;

activities were well planned, interesting, and easy to understand.

3. Children's Attitudes measured over the three years indicated that

children liked bilingual (Spanish and English) television shows;

children understood the segments in both languages;

the series prompted participation in word repetition and singing;

Agapito was the most popular character.

4. Parents' Attitudes obtained in the second and third years' evaluations indicated that

parents were in favor of a bilingual television series for primary school children;

the teaching of Mexican-American customs was deemed important;

pride in the Mexican-American culture and improvement in Spanish were thought to be positive effects;

about one-third of the parents watched "Carrascolendas."

Project Management

It may be recalled that in each of the three years a general evaluation was made of the overall management operation in the production dissemination of the series. Generalizations drawn across these three years were as follows:

1; Effective publicity and dissemination on a national scale has been consistently lacking, particularly with regard to Mexican-American populations.

2. Teacher workshops should be made available nationally to provide information about and encourage greater use of "Carrascolendas"

3. Planning time has not been adequate in the process of production activities and in the preparation of sites and consultants.

4. Limiting the number of programs on which viewers are tested would allow for variance in broadcast dates.

5. In the first year, role delineation needed more precise specification for the project's staff.

Ad Hoc Findings

At several junctures in the project, specific studies were undertaken of questions that arose during the regularly scheduled evaluations. The more important conclusions from these studies are as follows:

1. General measures of self-concept showed no effect.

2. Second-year gains were independent of the language dominance of the child.

3. Teachers' attitudes were tied to their bilingualism in some respects.

4. Teachers fluent in Spanish conducted more "Carrascolendas"-related activities and perceived the program's objectives better.

SPECIAL ASPECTS OF CULTURALLY
TARGETED EDUCATIONAL TELEVISION

Let us now look at the problem from a broader view—that of educational programming for particular ethnic or subcultural groups, of which the "Carrascolendas" series is an example.

The Importance of Self-concept

One of the most often discussed objectives of "Carrascolendas" was improvement of the children's self-concept. The various attitudinal assessments obtained from teachers and parents often referred to this as one of the major contributions of the program. And as was just summarized in Table 10.1, the measures of self-concept, based on behavioral objectives, provided some evidence of success in the third-year evaluation. However, as discussed in Chapter 9, when the attempt was made to develop a general measure of self-concept, one more in line with conceptual definitions, the results did not discriminate between viewers and nonviewers of "Carrascolendas."

Some recognition must be given to the problem of the definition of self-concept. As discussed in Chapter 9, there are a variety of definitions, and although there is some degree of consensus, few definitions easily fit a measurable specification.* There is also disagreement about the extent to which self-concept is developed before adolescence. It might be the case that in the five-, six-, and seven-year olds (the ages studied here) self-concept is only evolving in very rudimentary forms. Obviously, unless these rudimentary forms can be sufficiently defined, we can never hope to measure them accurately. If self-concept is a basic dimension of a child's personality, it is presumptuous to think that 13 or 14 hours of television programming, a small percentage of the child's 900 or so waking hours in a ten-week period, would have any major effects on a basic personality trait. To be even more exact about it, if we assume that only an average of two minutes out of each 30 minute program format were given over to self-concept, one would be even less likely to expect major effects on this trait. Still, it should be noted that when behavioral objectives in the self-concept area were considered, the program was sometimes found to have effects. These were not basic personality traits but such ability items as knowing one's name or attitudes such as feeling positive about oneself.

If it is assumed that self-concept is a viable objective for culturally targeted educational programming, several arguments can be made in its support. For one thing, the types of materials and experiences that presumably have an effect upon a child's self-concept lend themselves particularly well to the television medium. Thus if we were to argue whether mathematics or self-concept might best benefit from televised instruction, chances are that more arguments could be made for the advantages of television with the latter than with the former. The teacher is an important variable in affecting self-concept. Certainly, many of the strategies that teachers learn for dealing with the young child may influence his self-concept, but without specialized training in this area and a knowledge of the heritage and attitudes of a particular subculture, it is doubtful that a teacher can be very effective in this area. One bit of secondary evidence in the "Carrascolendas"

---

*See Chapter 9 for sample definitions.

project was the consistent effect of the program in the area of history/ culture. As can be seen in Table 10.1, this was an area of behavioral objectives that usually showed significant differences between viewers and nonviewers. It could be argued that, more than any other cluster of behavioral objectives, history/culture incorporated knowledge that was particularly relevent to self-concept.

Combining the advantages of the television medium with proper strategies in the classroom would make maximal use of culturally targeted educational television. Since the inception of the War on Poverty, there has been a shift from the philosophy of "getting the child ready for the school" to the more recent one of "getting the school ready for the child." The use of culturally targeted television programming is one way that the school environment can reflect the cultural heritage and values of the child and present them to him in a dynamic and reinforcing sense.

This discussion was meant to center upon several practical points. First, in looking over the three years' experience with "Carrascolendas," although there is evidence that the program was effective in various knowledge areas, we believe that its effects and potential impact in the area of self-concept and history/culture are particularly important. Many educators agree that the environment of the school is most alien to the minority-group child. Considerable argument can be made also that adaptation to a child's cultural background is one of the weakest areas of teacher preparation. In short, the practical implication is that if culturally targeted programming is to be developed for the schools, instruction in self-concept and history/culture are objectives that may benefit best from the advantages of the television medium. At the same time such televised instruction should aid us in overcoming some of the shortcomings of the schools and the teachers in meeting the needs of minority-group children.

Language and Bilingual Children's Television

As was noted in Table 10.1, language skills was one of the test areas that most consistently showed gains across the three years of the project. Such gains were indicated in terms of specific skill objectives in the second- and third-year evaluations in both the Spanish and English areas. In the first-year evaluation there were gains in terms of a separate measure of fluency in the children's interviews. We have thought that these gains were particularly important because language, itself, acts as a gatekeeper in perception of televised educational materials. That is, the child's basic linguistic abilities filter what he is able to perceive verbally from the televised presentation. This notion of language as a gatekeeper stems from an earlier project by the senior author where it was noted that children from lower-status families appeared to attend more to the visual aspects of a televised presentation, whereas children in middle-status families seemed to perceive more of the aural or verbalized content of the presentation.[1]

Language thus takes on a doubly important purpose as a behavioral objective in a series such as "Carrascolendas." First, the language of the series must be at the level of linguistic competency of the child viewer so that it can convey the instructional material. Second, if the instructional material can itself increase a child's linguistic abilities to some practical degree, it should have the effect of increasing his ability to learn other materials from the series. There has been a general consensus that language abilities are one of the most distinguishing features separating children of lower-socioeconomic-status families from their middle-class counterparts.[2] This is particularly true when the language abilities are confounded by problems of bilingualism (for example, Mexican-American) or bidialectalism (for example, black American). A number of lines of inquiry into this area were prompted by the British sociologist Basil Bernstein, who maintained that children from lower-status families (in Great Britain, at least) learned a style of home language that, although well developed in itself, was different from the language of the school, and hence impeded communication and learning in the academic environment.[3] These are not dialects but styles of language that Bernstein calls the restricted and elaborated codes, respectively.

Although Bernstein's hypothesis has been applied in the interpretation of language differences among children in the United States, differences of bilingualism and bidialectalism have not been taken into account. Also, many of the applications in the United States have incorporated the elaborated code as a more highly developed version of a restricted code, which may not be the case. In most of the senior author's prior writings,[4] it has been emphasized that differences between restricted and elaborated codes are more differences in styles and functions of speech than differences along a single continuum of complexity. That is, the variations that we see among children from different social classes are more those of linguistic and communication differences than deficits. If this position is assumed, then language instruction for children whose speech does not fit the school environment should build upon the home language rather than assume that a child is simply deficient in language development. Put another way, the "difference" assumption should prompt the type of instruction that shows contrast between home and school styles of speech and should emphasize the kinds of speech that are most effective in a given communication situation.

We suggest that televised language instruction, although incorporating linguistic details such as pronunciation and grammatical forms, should focus more on the concept of <u>mode of speech</u>. Here the mode of speech refers to the types of discourse used to meet the demands of different communication situations, such as interrogation, direction giving, explanation, and the like. Although grammatical details separate these styles of speech, it is the function of the style of speech in meeting the demands of the communication situation that is important, not the individual grammatical details.

Assuming the above point of view, it has seemed particularly important to argue that educational television, in focusing on language development, should attempt to portray speech in its most functionally relevant sense to the child. Thus while drills in phoneme/grapheme relationships or the presentation of simple vocabulary may be useful occasionally, the medium of television may have its most salient effect on a child's language learning if he experiences forms of speech used functionally in different communication contexts. This means that speech should be presented in a context of natural use, with numerous examples by characters with whom the children can identify. This seems particularly important in the instruction of the functional use of two languages by the bilingual individual. Thus, for the Mexican-American child, situations of speech should be presented as realistically as possible in the television medium, showing how bilingual individuals function in our society, and particularly how bilingualism is an asset when variation in communication situations demand it. It is probably just as important to communicate to the Mexican-American child the differences in context that prompt use of Spanish as against English as it is to present the grammatical details of the two languages to him.

Another important consideration in dealing with a bilingual child is the possibility of confusing the kind of code or home/school talk distinction that we mentioned earlier with language differences. Although this point will be debated by some, in our experience the Spanish used by the Mexican-American children we have studied is primarily a style of home talk. This does not mean that it is any less a complex form of language. It is a style used more for informal social communication among family and peers. This mode of Spanish, like the style of English that serves the same kind of home talk purpose, has distinctions when compared with what we have called school talk, or a more formal Spanish. Examples of home talk used often that differ from school talk follow:

Home Talk	School Talk	English
¿<u>Vistes</u> eso?	¿<u>Viste</u> eso?	Have you seen that?
Tengo que ir pa'l doctor.	Tengo que ir al doctor.	I have to go to the doctor.

170

Thus in dealing with the bilingual Mexican-American child there are differences, not only in contexts requiring Spanish and English, but between informal and formal situations. We cannot expect the child with the usual Spanish home talk repertoire to understand immediately how we move to a more formal use of Spanish in the academic environment unless the distinctions of speech style as well as language are communicated.

Another important point in planning the linguistic aspects of children's television is that materials promote the active involvement of the child in the viewing situation. Most commercial television, particularly that geared to adult entertainment tastes, promotes a very passive role on the part of the viewer. That is, the viewer is seldom challenged to respond in any way to materials presented on the television—they "do it for him." In fact, much of adult television—particularly crime and action programming—appears to have a catharsis effect. The viewer experiences emotional arousal, but with no overt activity on his part.

By contrast, most of our research, and some of the research on "Sesame Street," indicates that the more actively a child can participate while a viewer of the program, the greater effects the program will have on him. In the case of "Carrascolendas," such activity can be viewed in terms of children actively responding to the television set when they are encouraged to repeat words, when they are asked questions by a character in a skit, or, particularly, when they are encouraged to sing along with a musical presentation. Such activity heightens the level of attention to, and perception of, the program content. It is particularly important to see activity incorporated as a formal part of the instruction. Teachers can prepare the children to view a program, then have supplementary instructional activities that follow viewing. In our second year's evaluation we found that activities enhanced achievement of the behavioral objectives. In short, then, it seems to be an important planning principle that children's television should attempt to elicit as much active linguistic participation from the child viewer as possible. This includes warm-up and follow-up activities.

The summary point of this discussion is that language, along with self-concept and history/culture is another important instructional objective for bilingual children's television. In short, (1) language has a gatekeeping function on what the child can learn; (2) language both in style and tongue (Spanish-English) is one of the major factors that separate Mexican-American children from the mainstream school system; (3) the presentation of examples of language function—that is, how language varies according to communication contexts—is an objective well suited to the television medium; and (4) television can promote active use of language.

We are arguing that language be presented in a realistic and naturalistic sense in children's television. For bilingual children, in particular, contrasts of communication contexts should be presented along with the variations in which style of a language is used in terms of the informal/formal continuum. It may be just as important to illustrate for Mexican-American children the differences between informal and more formal speech as it is the differences between Spanish and English, and especially how each varies according to the demands of communication contexts.

Adaptation to the Subculture

One of the distinguishing features of "Carrascolendas," as compared with other instructional television programs for young children, is that it is targeted primarily to a particular ethnic group in the United States. Whereas "Sesame Street" is targeted to the so-called disadvantaged child of varying ethnicities, "Carrascolendas" is a program of Mexican-American content specifically targeted to Mexican-American children. In this respect it is a more specialized and culturally targeted program than "Sesame Street."

Even though the focus of "Carrascolendas" is on Mexican-Americans, there is far more heterogeneity in this population than one might think. While the details of such heterogeneity can be found elsewhere,[5] differences in the Mexican-American population include factors of age, urbanization, education, and socioeconomic status. These characteristics vary together to differentiate Mexican-American families of lower social status, who live in rural areas and primarily use Mexican Spanish, from families who have within the last generation moved to urban areas, had the benefit of more education, and are earning higher incomes. The more a family can be identified with the former group, the more Spanish will be the dominant language in the home, and the more a program of bilingual education is needed so that language will not be a barrier to the child's learning in school.

By contrast, the more a child is identified with the family in the latter classification, the less the child will use Spanish as compared with English, and probably the less he will be aware of cultural traditions and attitudes. In short, when a particular program segment is targeted to Mexican-American children, it must overcome substantial differences in the children's ability to understand Spanish, their knowledge of cultural conditions, and their attitudes toward the Mexican-American subculture. It should be emphasized also that the use of Spanish among Mexican-Americans not only varies substantially in terms of the degree of bilingualism between Spanish and English, but in dialects and colloquialisms used in different regions of the United

States. Common usage in Mexico for truck is camión, but many
Mexican-Americans have borrowed the English word and begun to
use the word troca. Other colloquialisms often used are:

to button - abotonar, abrochar
grass - sacate, césped, pasto, hierba, la yarda
you're welcome - no hay de que, de nada
dress -vestido, túnico

The word for sock varies in different locations and media and calcetín
are often used. However, the latter word has been mispronounced so
often, that saquetín is used frequently.

In the most practical sense, the, bilingual programming for
Mexican-American children must strike a balance between uses of
the Spanish language that have a degree of universality among this
subgroup in the United States and assumptions about cultural traditions
and attitudes. The results of the attitude questionnaires from teachers
and parents indicated that "Carrascolendas" has been moderately successful in this respect. There have been few objections to either the
language used in "Carrascolendas" or the cultural materials or attitudes
presented in the program.

In each year's evaluation of "Carrascolendas," children's attitudes
toward the material sometimes differed substantially from adult attitudes. This was particularly the case as segments depicted Mexican-
American children in some degree of cultural assimilation into the
Anglo society of the United States. Children seldom objected to these
materials.

One subjective view that we have developed over the past three
years is that the more materials in the program deal with the everyday
trials and tribulations of simply existing as a child or as a human being,
the more universal are these themes, and the more they tend to appeal
to a wide range of children and adults. Thus such concepts as love,
surprise, endurance, creativity, patience, and the like, which were
expressed in "Carrascolendas" within a bicultural or Mexican-American
setting, have a universal message and appeal for all children and adults.

One further question along this line is whether a bilingual Spanish-
English program like "Carrascolendas" would have utility with Spanish-
speaking groups in the United States other than Mexican-Americans.
Unfortunately, the circumstances for evaluation over the past three
years did not provide for investigation of the generalization of this
program to other groups. It has been suggested by several Puerto
Rican consultants that the difference between a Puerto Rican child in
New York City and a Mexican-American child in Arizona, even though
both may speak Spanish, is far greater than the difference between
the Puerto Rican child and his peers from different ethnic groups in

New York City. Thus, although language may be a common factor, urbanization, various aspects of cultural heritage, and the current differences in everyday problems may reduce the program's potential effectiveness with Spanish-speaking children other than Mexican-Americans. However, this is one aspect of "Carrascolendas" that bears objective research.

Three approaches to increasing the generality of "Carrascolendas" to other Spanish-speaking groups are as follows: (1) develop segments that include mixtures of different Spanish-speaking children where the topic of the segment reflects their differences; (2) develop segments that are basic to a child's everyday existence (as mentioned above) and do not identify a particular Spanish-speaking group; (3) edit programs to include more Puerto Rican segments when shown to that population, more Mexican-American segments for that population, and so on. In our experience, it seems possible to overcome the language differences among Spanish-speaking groups since, unless a particular subgroup identification is made, both vocabulary and accent can be generalized enough so as not to mark the program as being geared to one group or another.

Our main point here is that "Carrascolendas" has represented an example of culturally targeted educational television, and our experiences with it could be generalized to other such projects that might take this focus. However, even with cultural targeting, there is substantial heterogeneity among Mexican-Americans and this must be considered in programming. Further, although the Spanish language may link certain groups in the United States, the similarities may end there. Differences in background geographic areas, living conditions, and political content tend to accentuate differences among Spanish-speaking groups.

ACCOUNTABILITY IN CHILDREN'S EDUCATIONAL TELEVISION

The results of our three years' experience in evaluating "Carrascolendas" suggest a number of planning guidelines for assessing the accountability of children's television programming. By accountability we mean the relationship of the stated objectives of a project to learning gains that can be objectively assessed. Although we have not had a financial analysis included in the activities reported in this document,[6] there has been extensive experience with some of the basic ingredients of an accountability approach.

Behavioral Objectives

One generalization is that if a person is to make claims concerning the impact of a children's program that will in any way be subject to an accounting, objectives must be in terms of identifiable and measurable behaviors. Such behaviors can include attitudes so long as there is agreement on how measurement will be made. If such objectives are a new concept to the television producer, then he can be quite adequately guided by referring to the body of literature now available on the nature of instructional or behavioral objectives.[7] In the main, this literature indicates that a behavioral objective specifies a particular segment of desired behavior and defines it unambiguously, so that the behavior lends itself to measurement. If the criteria for behavioral objectives are followed, then such objectives form a common language among a program proposer, the producer, the educational planners, the script writers, the director, the teachers who may use the program in their classes, and the evaluators who will assess the program's accountability. In our own thinking, any proposed programming for children that does not have behavioral objectives can never be held accountable for its effects.

SUMMATIVE AND FORMATIVE EVALUATION

Given planning based upon behavioral objectives, evaluation can be undertaken in several forms. Most important to us, because of the nature of the required evaluations of Title VII programs, was the summative evaluation. After the series has been presented and viewed, we try to see what the summative effects have been. On the other hand, there is formative evaluation, where interim assessments are undertaken to facilitate the program development in its formative stages. In summative evaluation children may be pre- and posttested before and after an entire program series; in formative evaluation children may be pre- and posttested (or only posttested) following the presentation of an individual segment or segments. The study described in Chapter 9, which involved comparison of music and art styles, was an example of a formative evaluation.

Baseline Data

One particularly important use of behavioral objectives is that they will force the program planners to determine the children's competencies and needs in various instructional areas. That is to say, they prompt the need of baseline data: What should their next step in learning be? Any program that claims to be focused on a series of behavioral objectives should present arguments supporting these particular behavioral objectives as optimal for children in the population of the target audience.

Standardized Measures

One consistent question raised about evaluations of "Carrascolendas" was our lack of standardized measures. Why not, for example, assess the effects of "Carrascolendas" in terms of achievement tests routinely used in first and second grades, or even in terms of IQ tests? Throughout the project we argued that such tests were apt to be misleading in that the television series was only a small fraction of the child's total experience during a ten-week period, and we would not expect it to have overall effects on broad aspects of educational achievement, let alone IQ.

One analogy frequently used in discussing this point was that if we were to introduce orange juice into a children's breakfast program, we would not expect the addition to that one factor to result in gross effects like overall growth of the child or major weight gain. If we wanted to determine the effects of orange juice we might ask first whether the vitamins present in the orange juice were assimilated by the child's body. This question is akin to the kind of criterion-referenced evaluation used in the assessment of "Carrascolendas." If we expect programs in the series to have effects upon a priori specified learning behaviors, then at least the program should be held accountable for those particular effects. In short, to expect the program to be a distinguishing variable in whether children gain in IQ, or increase to a measurable extent in overall academic achievement, is a misleading approach to accountability.

Added to the above arguments are the special problems of considering standardized tests with minority-group children or children from families of lower socioeconomic status. There is the pressing question of the degree to which standardized tests confuse differences as deficits in minority-group populations, let alone whether the scoring criteria are statistically applicable to a population on which the tests were not originally standardized or developed.

In brief, then, our position has been to argue for a criterion-referenced evaluation both in a formative and summative sense in the development of children's television programming. We believe that such evaluations are particularly crucial in culturally targeted television where myths, misguided intentions, and political biases tend to blur the priorities of instruction. Sound evaluation is a powerful counteragent to such obstacles.

NOTES

1. Frederick Williams, "Social Class Differences in How Children Talk about Television," Journal of Broadcasting 13, no. 4 (Fall 1969).

2. See Frederick Williams, ed., Language and Poverty: Perspectives on a Theme (Chicago: Markham, 1970).

3. Ibid.

4. See Frederick Williams and Rita C. Naremore, "On the Functional Analysis of Social Class Differences in Modes of Speech," Speech Monographs 36 (June 1969).

5. Nicholas Valenzuela, Media Habits are Attitudes of Mexican-Americans: Surveys in Austin and San Antonio, and Frederick Williams, Nicholas Valenzuela, and Pamela Knight, Prediction of Mexican-American Media Habits and Attitudes (Austin: The University of Texas, Center for Communication Research, June 1973).

6. A fiscal analysis of "Carrascolendas" is forthcoming: Frank Korman, "Toward a Model of Cost Effectiveness Analysis for Educational Television," Unpublished Ph.D. dissertation, School of Communication, The University of Texas at Austin, 1973.

7. See, for example, Robert F. Mager, Preparing Instructional Objectives (Palo Alto, Calif.: Fearon, 1962).

EXAMEN EN ESPAÑOL [1:1]

Nombre_____ Nº. de identificación_____[2,3,4]

Segundo Examen [5:2]

Encierre uno de estos en un círculo

Orden [6] 1 Primero
           2 Segundo

Encierre uno de estos en un círculo

Grado: [7] 1 Primero
             2 Segundo
             3 Jardín Infantil

Preguntas para que el niño se sienta cómodo

¿Cómo te llamas?
¿Cuántos años tienes?
¿Cuántas personas hay en tu familia?

	Perfecto	Inducido	Parcial	Error; nada	Español	Mixto	Inglés
¿Qué idiomas hablas?* *español e inglés*	[8] 4	3	2	1	[9] 3	2	1
Pinta un tercio de la pelota. (pelota dividida en tercios)	[10] 4	3	2	1	[11:0]		

180

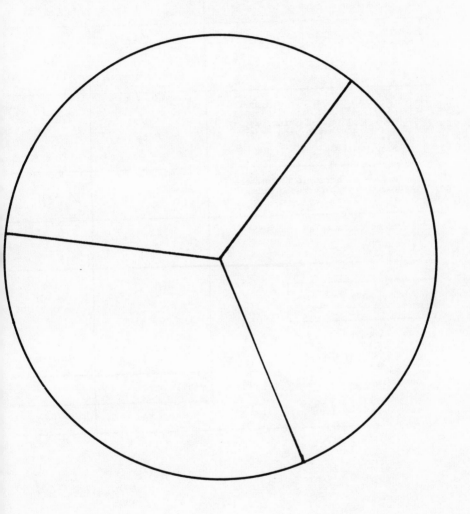

	Perfecto	Inducido	Parcial	Error; nada		Español	Mixto	Inglés
¿Cómo se llaman tu papá y tu mamá?*	[12]	4	3	2	1	[13] 3	2	1
Dime el nombre de una persona o de un animal que necesita que tú le ayudes.* *nombre de amigo, familia, animal, etc.*	[14]	4	3	2	1	[15] 3	2	1
Si vas a pintar un dibujo con un (a) amigo (a) y él (ella) tiene las brochas y tú tienes la pintura, ¿qué tienen que hacer para poder pintar?* *prestar, esperar**	[16]	4	3	2	1	[17] 3	2	1
¿Qué le pasa al mercurio en un termómetro, cuando hace mucho calor? *sube*	[18]	4	3	2	1	[19] 3	2	1
¿Qué número falta en el problema? $(1 + \underline{}\overset{3}{} = \boxed{4}\,)$	[20]	4	3	2	1	[21] 3	2	1

| Apunta a cada persona, y después a cada cosa. |

	Perfecto	Inducido	Parcial	Error; nada		
Haz una línea de cada persona a la cosa que hace.* carpintero - casa	[22]	4	3	2	1	[23:0]
panadero - pan	[24]	4	3	2	1	[25:0]
costurera - vestido	[26]	4	3	2	1	[27:0]

	Perfecto	Inducido	Parcial	Error; nada		Español	Mixto	Inglés

Apunta al panadero

¿Cómo se le dice a la persona que
hace pan?
panadero
(panadero, carpintero, costurera) — [28] 4 3 2 1 [29] 3 2 1

¿Con qué letra se escribe zorra?
z
(zorra, z, c, s) — [30] 4 3 2 1 [31:0]

¿Con qué letra se escribe burro?
b
(burro, b, v) — [32] 4 3 2 1 [33:0]

Apunta al niño

¿En qué cuarto se baña este niño?
el cuarto de baño
(el cuarto de baño, la recámara, la
sala, la cocina) — [34] 4 3 2 1 [35:0]

¿En qué cuarto duerme este niño?
la recámara
(el cuarto de baño, la recámara, la
sala, la cocina) — [36] 4 3 2 1 [37:0]

¿Qué le pasa a una pelota cuando se
avienta hacia arriba?*
se cae — [38] 4 3 2 1 [39] 3 2 1

¿Cuál tiene el mayor número de objetos?
(7 manzanas, 4 plátanos) — [40] 4 3 2 1 [41:0]

	Perfecto	Inducido	Parcial	Error; nada		Español	Mixto	Inglés

¿Cuál nos dice dónde estamos?
  la brújula
(termómetro, reloj, brújula, taza)   [42] 4 3 2 1   [43:0]

Apunta a la brújula

¿Qué es esto?
  brújula   [44] 4 3 2 1   [45] 3 2 1

Apunta a cada dibujo, y
después a la palabra

¿Cuál dibujo es igual a la palabra?
LLAVE - llave, vestido, teléfono   [46] 4 3 2 1   [47:0]

¿Cuál dibujo es igual a la palabra?
MUÑECA - muñeca, sombrero, limón   [48] 4 3 2 1   [49:0]

¿Cuál dibujo es igual a la palabra?
ZAPATOS - zapatos, flores, llave   [50] 4 3 2 1   [51:0]

¿Cuál dibujo es igual a la palabra?
GATO - gato, leche, dientes   [52] 4 3 2 1   [53:0]

¿Cuál dibujo es igual a la palabra?
VACA - vaca, hombre, oso   [54] 4 3 2 1   [55:0]

Apunta a cada conjunto, y
después a cada numeral   [56] 4 3 2 1   [57:0]

Haz una línea de cada conjunto al   [58] 4 3 2 1   [59:0]
numeral con que va.*
(5 pelotas, 3 perros, 8 sombreros -
5, 3, 8)   [60] 4 3 2 1   [61:0]

3

8

5

	Perfecto	Inducido	Parcial	Error; nada		Español	Mixto	Inglés

Te voy a decir una adivinanza, a ver
si la sabes: Una vieja larga y seca
que le escurre la manteca.
¿Qué es?
una vela   [62] 4 3 2 1   [63] 3 2 1

Apunta a la madera

¿Qué es esto
madera, palos, leña, tabla, etc.   [64] 4 3 2 1   [65] 3 2 1

¿Cuál se quiebra fácilmente?
vidrio
(piedra, madera, hierro, vidrio)   [66] 4 3 2 1   [67:0]

¿Cuál es tu dirección?*   [68] 4 3 2 1   [69] 3 2 1

¿Cómo se llama la tienda dónde se
compra carne?
carnicería   [70] 4 3 2 1   [71] 3 2 1

Repite* -
    Ahora vamos a jugar.   [72] 4 3 2 1   [73:0]

Repite -
    Tengo cuatro dedos en esta mano.   [74] 4 3 2 1   [75:0]

NO MARQUE AQUI

[76:]   [77:1]   [78:3]   [79:8]

[1:1]   [2,3,4:]   [5:2]   [6:]   [7:]

187

	Perfecto	Inducido	Parcial	Error; nada		Español	Mixto	Inglés

¿Cuál de estas letras es la /t/?
   t
(s l u t k)

[8] 4 3 2 1   [9 :0]

¿Cuál de estas letras es la /k/?
   qu
(qu x z r b)

[10] 4 3 2 1   [11:0]

¿Cuál de estas letras es la /g/?
   g
(x g j c n)

[12] 4 3 2 1   [13:0]

¿Cuál de estas cosas es diferente?
   el animal
(botella, animal, foco)

[14] 4 3 2 1   [15] 3 2 1

¿A quién vas a ver cuando estás muy
 enfermo(a)?*
   doctor, enfermera

[16] 4 3 2 1   [17] 3 2 1

¿Qué número falta?
   7
(5 6 _ 8 9 10)

[18] 4 3 2 1   [19] 3 2 1

   Apunta al niño bajo

¿Cómo es este niño, alto o bajo?
   bajo
(un niño alto y un niño bajo)

[20] 4 3 2 1   [21] 3 2 1

Báilame "La Raspa."*

[22] 4 3 2 1   [23:0]

Termina esto:

[24] 4 3 2 1   [25:0]

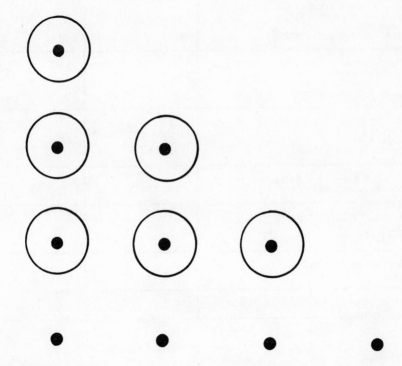

	Perfecto	Inducido	Parcial	Error; nada		Español	Mixto	Inglés
Cántame una de estas canciones en español:* La Vieja Inés La Víbora de la Mar San Serafín del Monte Juego Limpio Tengo Una Muñeca	[26] 4	3	2	1	[27] 3	2	1
¿Cuál de estas tres cosas empieza con el sonido /e/? *escoba* (escoba, iglesia, caballo)	[28] 4	3	2	1	[29:0]		
¿Cuál de estas tres cosas empieza con el sonido /t/? *tigre* (tigre, iglesia, perro)	[30] 4	3	2	1	[31:0]		
¿Cuál de estas tres cosas empieza con el sonido /s/? *zapatos* (zapatos, flores, jabón)	[32] 4	3	2	1	[33:0]		
¿Qué forma tiene una tortilla? *círculo, redondo*	[34] 4	3	2	1	[35] 3	2	1
Completa: AEIOU, El burro ____ ____ ____ *sabe más que tú*	[36] 4	3	2	1	[37] 3	2	1
¿Cuántos ojos tienes? *dos*	[38] 4	3	2	1	[39] 3	2	1
Haz una línea de un punto al otro.*	[40] 4	3	2	1	[41:0]		

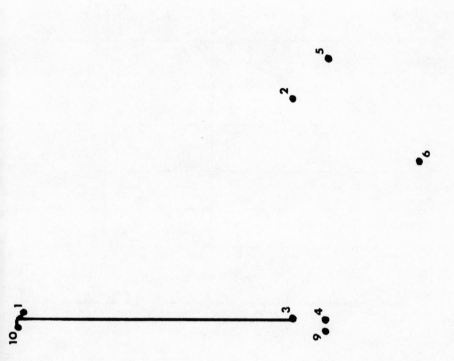

	Perfecto	Inducido	Parcial	Error; nada		Español	Mixto	Inglés
¿Cómo se le dice a las cáscaras de huevo que tienen confeti? *cascarones*	[42]	4	3	2	1	[43] 3	2	1
¿Qué se hace con los cascarones?* (se quiebran sobre la cabeza)	[44]	4	3	2	1	[45] 3	2	1
¿Qué es esto?* *piñata* (piñata)	[46]	4	3	2	1	[47] 3	2	1
Pon los dibujos en dos conjuntos. (3 osos grandes, 2 osos chicos)	[48]	4	3	2	1	[49:0]		
¿Cuál conjunto tiene más? *los osos grandes*	[50]	4	3	2	1	[51:0]		

[76:]   [77:2]   [78:3]   [79:8]

	Encierre uno de estos en un círculo
Evalúe la fluidez del niño durante el examen.	[76] 4 Buena 3 Aceptable 2 Poca 1 Nada

CONTINÚE EN LA PRÓXIMA PÁGINA

Child's Name_____ I.D. Number_____[2,3,4]

Post-test [5:2]

| CIRCLE ONE | | CIRCLE ONE |

Order: [6] 1 First
             2 Second

Grade Level: [7] 1 First
                   2 Second
                   3 Kindergarten

| QUESTIONS TO ASK CHILD TO |
| PUT HIM AT EASE |

What is your name?

How old are you?

How many people are in your family?

	Perfect	Prompted	Partial	Wrong; none		English	Mixed	Spanish
What languages do you speak?*	[8] 4	3	2	1	[9] 3	2	1
Which of these names is the name of a place: armadillo, San Antonio, mosquito? *San Antonio*	[10] 4	3	2	1	[11] 3	2	1

193

	Perfect	Prompted	Partial	Wrong; none		English	Mixed	Spanish
Barbecue is a word that was once a Spanish word which we now use as an English word. Tell me another Spanish word that is now used as an English word.*	[12] 4	3	2	1	[13]	3	2	1
What is the difference between these two jars?* (visual - one full jar; one empty jar)	[14] 4	3	2	1	[15]	3	2	1
Now I want you to ask me a question. Ask me if my friend walks to school.* *uses does*	[16] 4	3	2	1	[17]	3	2	1
Put these figures back to back. (objects - two plastic human figures)	[18] 4	3	2	1	[19 :0]			
Which one is on the left?	[20] 4	3	2	1	[21]	3	2	1
Tell me the name of one of these men. (photographs: Ishmael Soto-potter; Porfirio Salinas-painter; Tony Urbano-puppeteer)	[22] 4	3	2	1	[23]	3	2	1
What is his job? We would call him _ _____.*	[24] 4	3	2	1	[25]	3	2	1
José was invited to lunch at Tina's house. He left his house and got lost. He couldn't find Tina's house. He had to call Tina on the telephone and ask her where she lived. What could José have done so he wouldn't get lost?*	[26] 4	3	2	1	[27]	3	2	1

		Perfect	Prompted	Partial	Wrong; none		English	Mixed	Spanish
What is this? (visual - a piñata)	[28]	4	3	2	1	[29]	3	2	1
What are piñatas used for?* *celebrations, parties*	[30]	4	3	2	1	[31]	3	2	1
If you feel angry or mad, would it be better to hit somebody or to clean up your room?*	[32]	4	3	2	1	[33]	3	2	1
How are you like the girl/boy in this picture?* (visual - child of <u>opposite</u> sex)	[34]	4	3	2	1	[35]	3	2	1
How are you different from the girl/boy in this picture?* (visual - child of <u>opposite</u> sex)	[36]	4	3	2	1	[37]	3	2	1
If you are going to cross the street and there's a big puddle of water in front of you, tell me two ways you could get across.*	[38]	4	3	2	1	[39]	3	2	1
	[40]	4	3	2	1	[41]	3	2	1
Now we are going to say some words. Repeat each word after me: look/Luke*	[42]	4	3	2	1	[43]	3	2	1
bit/beat	[44]	4	3	2	1	[45]	3	2	1
best/vest	[46]	4	3	2	1	[47]	3	2	1

	Perfect	Prompted	Partial	Wrong; none		English	Mixed	Spanish
Point to child's own shoes								
Tell me, whose shoes are these?* *avoids mines*	[48] 4	3	2	1	[49] 3		2	1
Does this girl have on a dress?* (visual - girl)	[50] 4	3	2	1	[51] 3		2	1
Does this girl have on a raincoat?* (visual - girl) *uses doesn't*	[52] 4	3	2	1	[53] 3		2	1
Tell me how the earth is like an orange. *round, circle*	[54] 4	3	2	1	[55] 3		2	1
This is a rock. If we picked it up, it would be heavy. This next rock would be heavier. If we pick up all three rocks, this one would be the (what) ____.* *the heaviest* (visual - three rocks of different sizes)	[56] 4	3	2	1	[57] 3		2	1
This boy is in front of the man. Where is the man?* *in back of him* (visual - boy in front of man)	[58] 4	3	2	1	[59] 3		2	1
Put these pictures in order to show how honey is made.*	[60] 4	3	2	1	[61] 3		2	1
Tell me how honey is made.*	[62] 4	3	2	1	[63] 3		2	1

	Perfect	Prompted	Partial	Wrong; none		English	Mixed	Spanish
What are fences for?*	[64] 4	3	2	1	[65] 3	2	1
Look at these pictures. Where is the boy riding?* (visual - boy riding <u>on</u> bus)	[66] 4	3	2	1	[67] 3	2	1
Name four kinds of transportation.*	[68] 4	3	2	1	[69] 3	2	1
	[70] 4	3	2	1	[71] 3	2	1
	[72] 4	3	2	1	[73] 3	2	1
	[74] 4	3	2	1	[75] 3	2	1

```
                    DO NOT MARK IN THIS BOX

            [76: ]    [77:1]    [78:3]    [79:8]

        [1:2]    [2,3,4:  ]    [5:2]    [6:1]    [7: ]
```

	Perfect	Prompted	Partial	Wrong; none		English	Mixed	Spanish
What is in the suitcase? There isn't _____. *anything* (visual - empty suitcase)	[8] 4	3	2	1	[9] 3	2	1
This is a picture of a mouse. In this picture, there are two of them. There are two ____. (visual - 1 mouse; 2 mice)	[10] 4	3	2	1	[11] 3	2	1

	Perfect	Prompted	Partial	Wrong; none		English	Mixed	Spanish
If you are painting pictures with a friend and he wants to use the red paint when you are using it, what should you do?*	[12] 4	3	2	1	[13] 3	2	1
Tell me where the boy is. (visual - boy under table)	[14] 4	3	2	1	[15] 3	2	1
What are the names of your mother and father?*	[16] 4	3	2	1	[17] 3	2	1
Where is the girl sitting?* (visual - girl sitting on chair)	[18] 4	3	2	1	[19] 3	2	1
What is your address?*	[20] 4	3	2	1	[21] 3	2	1
What are bridges for?*	[22] 4	3	2	1	[23] 3	2	1
What do you do if you want to hear music on the radio? *turn it on* (visual - radio)	[24] 4	3	2	1	[25] 3	2	1
Tell me how to move a small boat in a pan of water.*	[26] 4	3	2	1	[27] 3	2	1

CIRCLE ONE

Please rate child's language fluency
in accordance with his performance
on this test.

[76] 4 High
      3 Medium
      2 Low
      1 No

[77:2]   [78:3]   [79:8]

GO ON TO THE NEXT PAGE.

198

TABLE 1

Site Characteristics

City	School	Type of Instruction	Percent of Mexican-American Pupils	Grade Level
Albuquerque	Armijo	Monolingual	78	K,1,2
	Coronado	Bilingual	90	K,1,2
	East San José	Bilingual	94	K,1,2
Edinburg	Lamar	Bilingual	90	K,2
	Central	Partly Bilingual	100	1
Lansing	Bingham	Monolingual	21	K,1,2
	Oak Park	Monolingual	39	1
Los Angeles	City Terrace	Bilingual	93	K,1,2
Pueblo	Bradford	Monolingual	75	K,1
	Hyde Park	Monolingual	73	K,1,2,3
	Bessemer	Monolingual	74	K,1,2,3
San Antonio	Collier I	Bilingual	96	K,1,2
	Columbia I	Bilingual	100	K,1,2
	Collier II	Monolingual		
	Columbia II	Monolingual		
Tracy	North	Monolingual	26	K,1,2
	Central	Monolingual	21	K,1,2
Tucson	Mission View	Bilingual	77	K,1,2

THE UNIVERSITY OF TEXAS AT AUSTIN
CENTER FOR COMMUNICATION RESEARCH
AUSTIN, TEXAS 78712

Office of the Director
Speech Building 214
AC 512—471-1095

November 13, 1972

Dear Teacher:

CARRASCOLENDAS, a bilingual television series is being shown nationally this year for the first time. In planning future programs and revisions, recommendations from teachers like yourself are very important.

We would appreciate your comments since you are in the unique position of being able to observe the children and their reactions to CARRAS-COLENDAS. The information you supply is invaluable.

We are enclosing a questionnaire and a stamped, self-addressed envelope. It would be very helpful to us if you would take five minutes to complete the information and return the questionnaire to us as soon as possible.

Sincerely,

Geraldine Van Wart

Geraldine Van Wart
Project Director

GVW:pab

Enclosure

CARRASCOLENDAS
TEACHER QUESTIONNAIRE
Please answer every question.

Name_____

School_____

City & State*_____[1,2]

Grade Level or Position _____[3]

Number in Class_____[4]

1. What is the approximate percentage of
the ethnic groups represented in your class?
Mexican-American ___% [5]*
Black ___% [6]
Anglo ___% [7]
Other ___% [8]
Total 100%

2. What percentage of the children in
your class speak Spanish? ___% [9]*

3. How often does your class watch
CARRASCOLENDAS? (Check one)
[10] 1___Every program
2___Twice a week
3___Once a week
4___Less than once a week
5___Never

4. Do you watch the program in color?
(Check one)
[11] 1___Yes
2___No, black and white
3___Do not watch the program

5. Is your television reception
satisfactory? (Check one)
[12] 1___Always
2___Often
3___Rarely
4___Never

6. Approximately how many students
watch the same television set? ____[13,14]

7. Have you heard of any other bilingual
children's television programs. (Check one)
[15] 1___No
*___Yes
If yes, give name_____

8. Has there been any publicity regarding
CARRASCOLENDAS in your area? (Check one)
[16] 1___Yes, newspaper
2___Yes, television and/or radio
3___Yes, national publication
4___Yes, local publication
5___None

9. How well do you speak Spanish? (Check
one)
[17] 1___Fluently
2___Moderately
3___Limitedly
4___English only

10. Are class activities conducted in
Spanish or English? (Check one)
[18] 1___Mostly in Spanish
2___Mostly in English
3___About half and half
4___No activities

11. Do you conduct any class activities
about CARRASCOLENDAS before or after viewing the program?
(Check one)   (Check one)
[19] 1___Always   [20] 1___Before only
2___Often   2___After only
3___Rarely   3___Some of both
4___Never   4___Neither

12. Usually, how do you explain the Spanish
segments to non-Spanish-speaking students?
(Check one)
[21] 1___You explain in English
2___Aide or parent explains
3___Spanish-speaking student explains
4___No explanations are made
5___No non-Spanish speakers are present

13. How often do you use the Teacher's
Guide? (Check one)
[22] 1___Every program
2___Most programs
3___Some programs
4___Never
5___Do not have one

14. How useful is the Teacher's Guide?
(Check one)
[23] 1___Very useful
2___Somewhat useful
3___Not too useful
4___Useless
5___Do not have one

15. Are the TV presentations clear enough so
that you understand the objectives without
looking in the Teacher's Guide? (Check one)
[24] 1___Always
2___Often
3___Rarely
4___Never

16. Is the subject content of CARRASCOLENDAS
appropriate for your students?

			Language Skills	
	(Check one)	(Check one)	(Check one)	(Check one)
	MATH [25]	SCIENCE [26]	SPANISH [27]	ENGLISH [28]
Always	1___	1___	1___	1___
Often	2___	2___	2___	2___
Rarely	3___	3___	3___	3___
Never	4___	4___	4___	4___

17. How valuable were the animation segments
presenting letter/sound relationships? (Check one)
[29] 1___Very valuable
2___Somewhat valuable
3___A little valuable
4___Of no value

18. Is the language level appropriate for
your students' understanding?

	SPANISH	ENGLISH
	(Check one)	(Check one)
	[30]	[31]
Always	1___	1___
Often	2___	2___
Rarely	3___	3___
Never	4___	4___

*Bracketed numbers and asterisks are for
coding purposes only.

203

19. Was the cultural and historical content beneficial to your students? (Check one)
[32] 1___Very much
2___Somewhat
3___A little
4___Not at all

20. Would you like to see the series repeated next year? (Check one)
[33] 1___Yes
2___No
3___No opinion

21. Would you like to see a follow-up program for your students at a more advanced level? (Check one)
[34]1___Yes
2___No
3___No opinion

22. In general, how well do you think that your students like CARRASCOLENDAS? (Check one)
[35] 1___Very much
2___Moderately
3___A little
4___Not at all

23. Do Spanish-speaking children engage in the Spanish and/or English audience-participation segments during the program?

	(Check one) SPANISH [36]	(Check one) ENGLISH [37]
Most engage all of the time	1___	1___
Most engage some of the time	2___	2___
A few engage most of the time	3___	3___
A few engage some of the time	4___	4___
Little participation	5___	5___
None present	6___	6___

24. Do English-speaking children engage in the Spanish and/or English audience-participation segments during the program?

	(Check one) SPANISH [38]	(Check one) ENGLISH [39]
Most engage all of the time	1___	1___
Most engage some of the time	2___	2___
A few engage most of the time	3___	3___
A few engage some of the time	4___	4___
Little participation	5___	5___
None present	6___	6___

25. Do Mexican-American children speak Spanish at school more often after watching the program? (Check one)
[40] 1___Yes, often
2___Yes, somewhat
3___No, not at all
4___No Mexican-American children present

26. Do the Mexican-American children in your class participate in class activities? (Check one)
[41] 1___Very much
2___Moderately
3___A little
4___Not at all
5___No Mexican-American children present

27. In general, how would you rate the Mexican-American children's self esteem in your classroom? (Check one)
[42] 1___High, proud of his Mexican-American heritage
2___Medium, accepts his heritage
3___Low, embarrassed by his heritage
4___No awareness of difference between Mexican-American heritage and any other ethnic group
5___No Mexican-American children present

28. Do you think that the Mexican-American children's self esteem or pride may benefit from watching CARRASCOLENDAS? (Check one)
[43] 1___Very much
2___Moderately
3___A little
4___Not at all
5___No Mexican-American children present

29. Are Mexican-American children willing to contribute experiences from their backgrounds during discussions pertaining to CARRASCOLENDAS? (Check one)
[44] 1___Yes, often
2___Yes, occasionally
3___No, never
4___No Mexican-American children present

30. Have non-Spanish speakers learned some Spanish after watching the program? (Check one)
[45] 1___Some Spanish
2___A little Spanish
3___No Spanish
4___No non-Spanish speakers present

31. Have children from other ethnic groups shown interest in learning more about Mexican culture after watching CARRASCOLENDAS? (Check one)
[46] 1___Yes, often
2___Yes, occasionally
3___No, never
4___No other ethnic groups present

32. Do non-Spanish-speaking students ask the Mexican-American children about CARRASCOLENDAS? (Check one)
[47] 1___Yes, often
2___Yes, occasionally
3___No, never
4___No non-Spanish speakers present

33. What do you think is the most significant effect of CARRASCOLENDAS on your students? _____
_____
_____

PLEASE WRITE ADDITIONAL COMMENTS ON REVERSE SIDE.
[78:3]
[79:2]

204

PLEASE HELP US MAKE YOUR CARRASCOLENDAS TEACHER GUIDE BETTER FOR YOU

Class composition (rough %):
___Mexican-American
___Black
___Anglo
___Other

How often do Spanish-speaking children in your class use Spanish?
___most of the time
___sometimes
___occasionally
___not at all

How well do you speak Spanish?
___fluently
___moderately well
___a little
___not at all

Grade level_____

How often do you watch the series?
___every program
___twice a week
___once a week
___less than once a week

How often do you use the Teachers' Guide?
___regularly
___often
___seldom
___not at all

What is the degree of Spanish instruction in your school?_____
_____
_____

PLEASE GIVE A RATING BY PLACING A CHECK MARK IN ONE OF THE BLANKS BELOW

As an aid in using Carrascolendas in my class, the guide helped me:
very much __:__:__:__:__:__:__ not at all

The guide was:
difficult to use __:__:__:__:__:__:__ easy to use

The activities were:
not well explained __:__:__:__:__:__:__ fully explained

The suggestions coordinated with my own class activities:
very well __:__:__:__:__:__:__ not very well

The activities seemed to encourage concept learning beyond simple verbalization of skills:
seldom __:__:__:__:__:__:__ often

PLEASE RATE THE FOLLOWING FEATURES OR SECTIONS OF THE GUIDE

	VERY USEFUL				NOT USEFUL
Capsule descriptions	___	___	___	___	___
Visuals	___	___	___	___	___
Music	___	___	___	___	___
Translations	___	___	___	___	___
Science	___	___	___	___	___
Math	___	___	___	___	___
Reading	___	___	___	___	___
Spanish language skills	___	___	___	___	___
English language skills	___	___	___	___	___
Self concept	___	___	___	___	___
History and culture	___	___	___	___	___

What changes would you make in the Teachers' Guide?
_____
_____
_____

Please fold this sheet, staple, and mail as indicated on the reverse side. Thank you for your help.

USAGE SURVEY

Name:_____ School:_____

Address:_____ City, state, and zip code:_____

PLEASE ANSWER THE EIGHT QUESTIONS BELOW:

1. Total school enrollment:_____

2. Please indicate the number of classes per grade level:
   ___pre-K   ___Second   ___Fifth   ___nongraded classrooms
   ___Kindergarten   ___Third   ___Sixth   ___special education
   ___First   ___Fourth   ___7-12   ___other:_____

3. Percentage of ethnic groups represented in school:
   ___% Mexican-American   ___% Anglo   ___% Oriental
   ___% Black   ___% American Indian   ___% Other:_____

4. Does your school participate in a bilingual program? ___yes ___no

5. Is it funded by Title VII? ___yes ___no   Title I? ___yes ___no

6. Is CARRASCOLENDAS available in your area? ___yes ___no ___don't know

7. Are you planning to have classes viewing CARRASCOLENDAS? ___yes ___no ___don't know

   | If YES . . . . . | | If NO . . . . . |

   a. Please indicate the number of   Please indicate reasons for not
      classes viewing: watching CARRASCOLENDAS:
      ___pre-K   ___5   ___never heard of it before
      ___K   ___6   ___no TV available
      ___1   ___7-12   ___not available in your area
      ___2   ___nongraded classrooms   ___TV cable not available
      ___3   ___special education ___reception not satisfactory
      ___4   ___other:_____   ___no Spanish taught in school
                                          ___not interested
   b. Please indicate the number of addi- ___schedule conflict:_____
      tional classrooms which would view
      if TV's were available. _____   _____
                                          ___other:_____
   c. Have you ordered copies of CARRAS- _____
      COLENDAS Teacher Guide? ___yes
      ___no ___did not know about them

8. How did you learn about the series?
   ___superintendent's office   ___teacher   ___TV
   ___other principals   ___radio   ___magazine
   ___bilingual coordinator   ___newspaper   ___other:_____

PLEASE FOLD AND MAIL

CHILD ATTITUDE SURVEY - III

1. Do you watch TV at home? [4] 1___yes 2___no

    ┌─────────────────────────────────┐
    │   If NO, skip to question 3   │
    └─────────────────────────────────┘

2. What programs do you like to watch on TV? [5]
    1___CARRASCOLENDAS   5___Local program:_____
    2___Sesame Street   6___Cartoons
    3___The Electric Company   7___Other:_____
    4___Misterogers' Neighborhood

3. Do you like to watch TV at school?
            If YES [6] 0___Did not answer YES
                        1___I learn something (educational)
                        2___It's fun (entertainment)
                        3___I can see programs at school I can't see
                               at home
                        4___It's fun to watch TV with all the other
                               children
                        5___Don't know
                        6___Other:_____

            If NO [7] 0___Did not answer NO
                        1___Boring, not fun (not entertaining)
                        2___We don't watch many programs
                        3___I can't talk while watching the program
                        4___Too many people watching one set
                        5___Don't know
                        6___Other:_____
                        7___No TV at school

4. What languages do you think the TV shows should be in?
            [8] 1___Spanish 2___English 3___Both

5. Do you speak Spanish or English to your friends?
            [9] 1___Spanish 2___English 3___Both

6. Do you speak Spanish or English to your parents?
            [10] 1___Spanish 2___English 3___Both

7. Do you speak Spanish or English to your brothers and sisters?
            [11] 1___Spanish 2___English 3___Both 4___No brothers
                                                          or sisters
8. Do you speak Spanish or English to your teachers?
            [12] 1___Spanish 2___English 3___Both

9. Have you heard of a TV show called CARRASCOLENDAS?
    [13] 1___yes 2___no | If NO, do not continue |

10. Where do you watch CARRASCOLENDAS?
    [14] 1___don't watch 2___home 3___school 4___both

| If child does not watch CARRASCOLENDAS, do not continue |

11. Do you like CARRASCOLENDAS?
    If YES [15] 0___Did not answer YES
                 1___I like songs
                 2___I like characters
                 3___I like films
                 4___I like puppets
                 5___I like both Spanish and English in a program
                 6___Fun to watch (entertaining)
                 7___Other:_____

    If No [16] 0___Did not answer NO
                 1___Don't like songs
                 2___Don't like characters
                 3___Don't like puppets
                 4___Not entertaining
                 5___Can't understand parts of the program
                 6___Too many people watching one set
                 7___Other:_____

12. Do you understand when they speak Spanish on CARRASCOLENDAS?
    [17] 1___yes 2___no 3___sometimes 4___don't know

13. Do you understand when they speak English on CARRASCOLENDAS?
    [18] 1___yes 2___no 3___sometimes 4___don't know

14. Do you say the words when they flash on TV?
    [19] 1___yes 2___no 3___sometimes 4___don't know

15. Do you sing the songs with the TV?
    [20] 1___yes 2___no 3___sometimes 4___don't know

16. Do you like the songs? [21] 1___yes 2___no 3___some

17. Sing a song you learned on CARRASCOLENDAS. [22] 1_____
    | Write any response--title or first words, etc. | 2___no response
                                                        3___don't know

18. Additional remarks:
    1._____
    2._____

[78:3]
[79:7]

211

PARENT ATTITUDE SURVEY

Buenos días (Buenas tardes, noches). Habla (first and last name). Estoy trabajando en un proyecto para la Universidad de Texas y estamos haciendo unos estudios en diferentes ciudades. Si me permite unos minutos, le quisiera hacer unas preguntas.

Good morning (afternoon, evening). My name is (first and last name). I'm working on a project for the University of Texas and we are conducting surveys in various cities. If you have a few minutes, I would like to ask you a few questions.

^   ^   ^   ^   ^

¿Tiene hijos que ven televisión?

Do your children watch television?

This question is designed as an introduction for the respondent to become accustomed to the situation. Encourage him to talk here. It is not necessary to record his answer.

If, however, he states that he has no children or they do not watch any television at all, close the interview with the following:

Muchas gracias por haberme ayudado, pero tengo que hablar con padres de niños que ven televisión. Adiós.

Thank you for your time, but I need to interview par-ents whose children watch television. Goodbye.

¿Tiene hijos que ven el programa CARRASCOLENDAS en la escuela o en la casa? El programa comenzó en octubre y se ve en la estación _____ (nombre de la estación) a las _____ (hora).

Do your children ever watch, at home or at school, the children's program CARRASCOLENDAS, which began here on _____ (name of station) in October? It comes on at _____ (time).

If the respondent does not seem to recognize the name CARRASCOLENDAS, you can provide him with de-scriptive cues in order to establish the situation. All questions after this one must follow the form of the question which is printed.

---

[4]   1____No

2____Yes, at home

3____Yes, at school

4____Yes, both at home and at school

¿Cree que es importante tener un programa bilingüe de televisión para niños de escuelas elementales?

Do you think it is important to have a bilingual television program for primary school children?

If only yes or no, ask why?

YES [5]

0____Did not answer YES

1____Presents example of using Spanish language

2____Presents example of using Spanish and English both

3____Teaches Spanish

4____Teaches English

5____Other teaching areas presented in Spanish

6____Presents example of cultural items

*7____Other: _____

_____

_____

NO [6]

0____Did not answer NO

1____Don't want child to use Spanish

2____Doesn't need additional exposure to Spanish

3____Takes up school time

4____Don't think television is a good way to teach

5____Hearing Spanish on television would confuse child

6____Hearing English on television would confuse child

7____Don't like the two languages used together

*8____Other: _____

¿Qué idioma quiere que sus hijos hablen?

What language do you want your children to speak?

[7]

   1____Spanish and English both

   2____Spanish only

   3____English only

   4____Don't care

*5____Other:_____

_____

¿Cree que es importante enseñar algo acerca de la cultura méxico-americana?

Do you think it is important to teach Mexican-American culture?

YES, because [8]

   0____Did not answer YES

   1____Teaches him to be proud of his culture

   2____He learns that there are others like him

   3____Teaches others about Mexican-American culture

*4____Other:_____

_____

NO, because [9]

   0____Did not answer NO

   1____Not important

   2____Already has enough exposure

   3____Want him to get away from Mexican-American culture

*4____Other: _____

¿Ha visto usted CARRASCOLENDAS alguna vez? (¿Cuántas veces?)

Have you ever watched CARRASCOLENDAS? (How often?)

[10]

    1____NO*

    2____Don't know

    3____Yes, one time

    4____Two or three times

    5____Many times

    6____Almost always

    7____Always

    8____Heard it from another room

   *9____Other: _____

_____

---

*If NO, close as follows:

Muchas gracias por haberme ayudado. Adiós.

Thank you for answering these questions for me. Goodbye.

^   ^   ^   ^   ^

Turn to page 11 and fill in [21] and [22].

¿Cómo supo del programa CARRASCOLENDAS?

How did you hear about CARRASCOLENDAS?

[11]

    1____School

    2____Child

    3____Friend

    4____Newspaper or magazine

    5____Television

 *6____Other: _____

        _____

        _____

¿Cuál es su opinión de CARRASCOLENDAS?

What is your opinion of CARRASCOLENDAS?

LIKE, because [12]

   0_____Did not answer LIKE

   1_____It is a good program

   2_____It is entertaining

   3_____It uses Spanish

   4_____It uses Spanish and English both

   5_____General instructional value

   6_____Music is good

   7_____Presents Mexican-American culture

*8_____Other: _____

DON'T LIKE, because [13]

   0_____Did not answer DON'T LIKE

   1_____Not a good program

   2_____Don't like children to be exposed to Spanish

   3_____The Spanish isn't good

   4_____Too much entertainment, not enough teaching

   5_____Not enough Mexican-American features

   6_____Cultural presentations are poor

   7_____Instruction is poor

*8_____Other: _____

   9_____Don't know

¿Cuál es su opinión de las costumbres mexicanas que se presentan en los programas?

What do you think of the Mexican customs presented in the series?

LIKE, because [14]

   0____Did not answer LIKE

   1____Good presentations

   2____They are familiar to child

   3____Good for child to see them on television

   4____Teaches others about Mexican-American culture

 *5____Other: _____

             _____

             _____

DON'T LIKE, because [15]

   0____Did not answer DON'T LIKE

   1____Not enough treatment

   2____They are not authentic

   3____Want child to get away from Mexican-American customs

 *4____Other: _____

             _____

             _____

   5____No opinion

¿Le gusta el español que se usa en los programas?

Do you like the Spanish used in the program?

[16] 1____No

2____Yes

3____Don't know; not sure

¿Les ha ayudado el programa CARRASCOLENDAS a sus hijos a aprender mejor el español o el inglés?

Has watching CARRASCOLENDAS had any effect on your children learning Spanish or English?

[17] 1____No, neither

2____Don't watch often enough

3____Yes, Spanish

4____Yes, English

5____Yes, both Spanish and English

*6____Other: _____

_____

_____

7____Don't know

¿Qué cambios le gustaría que se hicieran en el programa?

What changes would you like to see in the series?

[18] 1____Speak in Spanish more

2____Speak in English more

3____More Mexican-American talent

*4____More of: _____

_____

*5____Less of: _____

_____

6____Wouldn't change it

7____Don't know

¿Qué otros resultados cree que CARRASCOLENDAS ha conseguido?

What other effects do you think CARRASCOLENDAS has had?

[19] 1____Pride in culture for Mexican-Americans

2____Teaches others about Mexican-Americans

3____Pride in speaking Spanish

4____Language improvement in Spanish

5____Language improvement in English

*6____Other: _____

_____

7____No effects

8____Don't know

¿Tiene algunos otros comentarios o sugerencias?

Do you have any other comments?

Please write comments one to a line and number them.

[20]   0____No comments

_____

_____

_____

_____

_____

_____

_____

NOTES ON INTERVIEW:

Sex of respondent:

[21]   1____Male

     2____Female

Special circumstances:

[22]   0____None

_____

_____

_____

_____

[78:3]
[79:4]

SELF CONCEPT TEST ITEMS

1. *If your mother is not at home at lunch time, can you make yourself a sandwich?*

    Si tu mamá no está en la casa a la hora de comer, ¿te puedes hacer tú solo un sandwich?

* 2. *Do you have anything that is yours and no one else's?*

    ¿Tienes una cosa que es solo tuya y no es de nadie más?

3. *If you are talking to a puppy, do you talk in Spanish?*

    Si hablas con un perrito, ¿le hablas en español?

4. *Do you ever go by yourself to visit a friend at his house?*

    ¿Vas solo algunas veces a ver a un amigo a su casa?

5. *Can you do one thing that nobody else can do?*

    ¿Puedes hacer algo que nadie más puede hacer?

6. *If you are on a deserted island, can you find food?*

    Si estás solo en una isla donde no hay otra persons, ¿puedes encontrar algo para comer?

* 7. *When you play like you're grown-up, how do you feel?*

    Cuando juegas como que eres una persona grande, ¿cómo te sientes?

8. *When you hear your teacher speak Spanish, how do you feel?*

    Cuando tu maestra habla español, ¿cómo te sientes?

9. *When you look at yourself in the mirror, how do you feel?*

    Cuando te miras en un espejo, ¿cómo te sientes?

10. *When you hear someone say your name wrong, how do you feel?*

    Cuando oyes a alguien que no dice tu nombre bien, ¿cómo te sientes?

*11. *When you hear your parents speak English, how do you feel?*

    Cuando oyes a tus papás hablar en inglés, ¿cómo te sientes?

*12. When you play with a friend who only speaks Spanish, how do you feel?

Cuando juegas con un amigo que solo habla español, ¿cómo te sientes?

13. When you are alone in a room, how do you feel?

Cuando estás solo en un cuarto, ¿cómo te sientes?

14. When you are learning something new in school, how do you feel?

Cuando estás aprendiendo una cosa nueva en la escuela, ¿cómo te sientes?

15. When you watch television in school, how do you feel?

Cuando ves televisión en la escuela, ¿cómo te sientes?

16. When you ask a friend to help you, how do you feel?

Cuando le pides a un amigo que te ayude, ¿cómo te sientes?

*17. When you talk in English, how do you feel?

Cuando hablas en inglés, ¿cómo te sientes?

*18. When you hear your parents speak Spanish, how do you feel?

Cuando oyes a tus papás hablar en español, ¿cómo te sientes?

19. When you eat lunch with your friends, how do you feel?

Cuando comes con tus amigos, ¿cómo te sientes?

20. When you learn new words in English, how do you feel?

Cuando aprendes palabras nuevas en inglés, ¿cómo te sientes?

21. If someone gives you a record of Spanish songs, how do you feel?

Si alguien te da un disco de canciones en español, ¿cómo te sientes?

22. When your teacher talks to your parents, how do you feel?

Cuando tu maestra habla con tus papás, ¿cómo te sientes?

23. When you learn new words in Spanish, how do you feel?

Cuando aprendes palabras nuevas en español, ¿cómo te sientes?

24. When you watch television and it's in English, how do you feel?

Cuando ves televisión y es en inglés, ¿cómo te sientes?

*25. When your parents are happy with your school work, how do you feel?

Cuando a tus papás les gusta el trabajo que haces en la escuela, ¿cómo te sientes?

26. When you talk in Spanish, how do you feel?

Cuando hablas español, ¿cómo te sientes?

27. When your mother asks you to help her at home, how do you feel?

Cuando tu mamá te dice que le ayudes en la casa, ¿cómo te sientes?

28. When you hear a song in Spanish, how do you feel?

Cuando oyes una canción en español, ¿cómo te sientes?

29. If someone gives you a taco instead of a hamburger, how do you feel?

Si alguien te da un taco en vez de una hamburguesa, ¿cómo te sientes?

30. When someone smaller than you knows the answer to a question, and you don't know the answer, how do you feel?

Cuando alguien más chico que tú sabe como contestar una pregunta, y tú no sabes como contestarla, ¿cómo te sientes?

31. When you make a mistake in front of your friends, how do you feel?

Cuando haces un error en frente de tus amigos, ¿cómo te sientes?

32. When you help a friend, how do you feel?

Cuando le ayudas a un amigo, ¿cómo te sientes?

33. When you break a toy at home, how do you feel?

Cuando rompes un juguete en tu casa, ¿cómo te sientes?

34. If someone wants to play with your toys, how do you feel?

Si alguien quiere jugar con tus juguetes, ¿cómo te sientes?

*35. When your teacher is happy with your school work, how do you feel?

Cuando a tu maestra le gusta el trabajo que haces en la escuela, ¿cómo te sientes?

36. When you play a trick on someone, and he gets hurt, how do you feel?

Cuando le haces algo malo a un amigo y le duels, ¿cómo to sientes?

*37. When you play with a friend who only speaks English, how do you feel?

Cuando juegas con un amigo que nada más habla inglés, ¿cómo te sientes?

38. When the teacher asks you a question and you don't know the answer, how do you feel?

Cuando tu maestra te pregunta algo y tú no sabes como contestar, ¿cómo te sientes?

39. When you watch television and it's in Spanish, how do you feel?

Cuando ves televisión y es en español, ¿cómo te sientes?

FREDERICK WILLIAMS is Professor and Dean of the Annenberg School of Communications at the University of Southern California. Formerly he was Director of the Center for Communication Research at the University of Texas, where the research reported in this monograph was coordinated.

Dr. Williams has published some 40 scholarly papers in the area of language and communication. He is author of Reasoning with Statistics (1968) and Language and Speech (1972) and is editor of and contributor to Language and Poverty (1970) and Normal Aspects of Speech, Hearing, and Language (1973). He holds M.A. and Ph.D. degrees from the University of Southern California.

GERALDINE VAN WART, currently with the Education Service Center in Austin, is evaluating the effects of "Carrascolendas" with its primary audience for the third year.

Ms. Van Wart, a Mexican-American who has lived and studied in Mexico and Venezuela, has taught Spanish to children in kindergarten through the sixth grade in Texas schools. She is coauthor of an elementary reading and exercise book, Leamos un Cuento, which is designed for children who have some speaking knowledge of Spanish.

Ms. Van Wart received her B.S. degree from the University of Houston with majors in Spanish and Elementary Education.

CHILDREN AND THE URBAN ENVIRONMENT:
A LEARNING EXPERIENCE: Evaluation of the
WGBH-TV Educational Project
                    Prepared by Marshall Kaplan, Gans,
                    and Kahn

CHILDREN'S TELEVISION COMMERCIALS:
A Content Analysis
                    Charles Winick, Lorne G. Williamson,
                    Stuart F. Chuzmir, Mariann Pezella
                    Winick
                    foreword by Paul F. Lazarsfeld

GETTING TO SESAME STREET: Origins of
the Children's Television Workshop
                    Richard M Polsky